DEVAUGH

CHA

OR

DIE

PURSUING YOUR POSSIBILITIES WITHOUT
SUCCUMBING TO YOUR REALITIES

Change or Die: Pursuing Your Possibilities Without Succumbing to Your Realities
Copyright © 2017 by Devaughn Kelly

All rights reserved. No part of this book may be reproduced in any form, stored in a retrieval system, or transmitted in any form by any means – electronic, mechanical, photocopy, recording, or otherwise – without permission in writing from the publisher, except in the case of brief quotations embodied in critical articles or reviews and as provided by United States of America copyright law.

Any Internet addresses (websites, blogs, etc.) printed in this book are offered only as references readily accessible by the public.

Scripture quotations marked HCSB are taken from the Holman Christian Standard Bible®, Copyright © 1999, 2000, 2002, 2003, 2009 by Holman Bible Publishers. Used by permission. Holman Christian Standard Bible®, Holman CSB®, and HCSB® are federally registered trademarks of Holman Bible Publishers.

Scripture quotations noted KJV are from the King James Version of the Holy Bible

Scripture quotations marked MSG are taken from *THE MESSAGE*, copyright © 1993, 1994, 1995, 1996, 2000, 2001, 2002 by Eugene H. Peterson. Used by permission of NavPress. All rights reserved. Represented by Tyndale House Publishers, Inc.

Scripture quotations taken from the New American Standard Bible® (NASB), Copyright © 1960, 1962, 1963, 1968, 1971, 1972, 1973, 1975, 1977, 1995 by The Lockman Foundation
Used by permission. www.Lockman.org

Scripture quotations taken from THE HOLY BIBLE, NEW INTERNATIONAL VERSION®, NIV® Copyright © 1973, 1978, 1984, 2011 by Biblica, Inc.® Used by permission. All rights reserved worldwide.

Scripture taken from the New King James Version®. Copyright © 1982 by Thomas Nelson. Used by permission. All rights reserved.

Scriptures taken from The Living Bible copyright © 1971 by Tyndale House Foundation. Used by permission of Tyndale House Publishers Inc., Carol Stream, Illinois 60188. All rights reserved. The Living Bible, TLB, and the The Living Bible logo are registered trademarks of Tyndale House Publishers.

Published by Devaughn Kelly Media and Motivation, 15630 West 7 Mile, Detroit, MI 48235 – D.KellyMM@gmail.com

I must thank God for his saving grace, his divine influence, and for giving me the gift of ministry through both spoken and now written word! I am so amazed, honored and flattered that he would choose me to be an agent of change for his people. All of the glory belongs to him, only the mistakes are mine.

I dedicate this work to the first visionary of my authorship... my fantastic wife Anshanett Kelly. I never imaged I would be an author – God placed this vision in you to bring a new gift out of me. Your love and support has meant more to me than I can say. You are my partner, my cheerleader, my editor and my agent! This journey has not been easy, but you've been with me every step of the way. This work would have never been started or completed without you. I believe this book will bless millions of people around the world, and it will have all started with you! Take a bow beautiful! God's not through with us by a long shot. This is only the beginning!

To my boys – my sons, Jorrell and Jaxon. You guys are my greatest achievement and my greatest inspiration! Don't ever withhold your gifts. The world is waiting! Dad loves you.

Darlynn (Greatest Mom any person could ask for), Jordan, Audrianna...I love you 3 so much! Thanks you for always being there. You mean the world to me!

Grandma Audrey Kelly, Auntie Chaney, Auntie Hazel (RIP), Auntie Jacky, Aaron & Mike (My Brothers for Life...I can't stand either of you! LOL!), Bishop J. Drew Sheard, First Lady Karen Clark Sheard, Pastor Tommy Vanover, First Lady Vivian Vanover, Linda Adams, Sherita Adams, Brian

Hariston, Daryl Jones, Dorinda Clark Cole, Teresa Cox...you all have either raised me, supported me, cared for me, protected me, or spoken great things over me...above all you've loved me...and I love you all in a special way!

Very special thanks to my Godfather. You've guided me through this process – same as you've guided me through manhood. Glynn Taylor Chisholm.

And to the rest of my family! Every husband, mother, father, brother, sister, Godparent, wife, child, cousin, aunt, uncle and friend. I love you all! Thank you for all that you do!

To the greatest church a pastor could ever have...The Valiant Church!!!! You guys are my amazing! Thank you for your love and support! You are truly a vision come to reality! You are the best church on the planet...the planet will soon find out! We are Brave...We are Strong...We are VALIANT!!!

Last but not least, to you the reader! Thank you for allowing God to minister to you through me! I truly believe these pages hold the words that will bring about the greatest and most beneficial changes your life has ever seen! You've changed my life just by picking up this book...it is my honor to return the favor!

CONTENTS

PREFACE

PART ONE: The Realization of Change

    CHAPTER ONE: Truth and Transparency with Yourself

    CHAPETR TWO: Truth and Transparency with People

    CHAPTER THREE: Truth and Transparency with God

    CHAPETR FOUR: You Will Never Be Ready

    CHAPTER FIVE: If You Can Change Why Haven't You

PART TWO: The Stress of Change

    CHAPTER SIX: Stressed Equals Blessed

    CHAPTER SEVEN: Stress – Pride, Purpose and People

    CHAPTER EIGHT: The Temporary Avoidance of Others

CHAPTER NINE: Stress Tests

CHAPTER TEN: Too Much Stress

CHAPTER ELEVEN: Why Am I Stressed

PART THREE: The Belief in Change

CHAPTER TWELVE: How Do I Change

CHAPTER THIRTEEN: The Ability to Change

CHAPTER FOURTEEN: Change Takes Confidence

CHAPTER FIFTEENEEN: It's Really Going to Happen This Time

PART FOUR: The Process of Change

CHAPTER SIXTEEN: The Way to Change

CHAPTER SEVENTEEN: Change Is in the Opposite Direction

CHAPTER EIGHTEEN: The Harsh Reality of Change

CHAPTER NINETEEN: Provoked to Change

PART FIVE: The Faith to Change

    CHAPTER TWENTY: Changed By Faith

    CHAPTER TWENTY ONE: The Faith to Fix What's Been Broken

    CHAPTER TWENTY TWO: Change What Seems Harmless

    CHAPTER TWENTY THREE: Setbacks Are Changes Too...Be Careful

PART SIX: The Results of Change

    CHAPTER TWENTY FOUR: The Moving Pieces of Change

    CHAPTER TWENTY FIVE: Change is Closer than You Think

    CHAPTER TWENTY SIX: Choose to Change

PREFACE

You may be wondering why an inspirational self help book, specifically one that is bible based, would have such a bold and dramatic title. After all, when we think of "change" we would like to think of it as something that brings about positive results - not dire consequences. We all want to feel inspired to change, and I do realize, at first glance the words "Change or Die" may seem to be more threatening than inspiring. But I assure you, there is a very essential and **life giving** message behind those words; a message I believe I have been called and commission to share with you.

As I have gone through life I have encountered individuals whose lives have been negatively impacted by a wide variety of issues. In spite of those issues causing major problems, those problems were strong enough to motivate those individuals to change. There are some people who actually believe that they can fix their lives by doing more of the negative things that have thrown their lives off track. I have known alcoholics who drink as a means of dealing with the problems their drinking continues to cause. I have encountered people who have used adultery as a means of dealing with problems in their marriage, seeking the affections of a spouse through the embrace of another. I have known individuals who have stayed committed to people who continually undervalue and mistreat them, hoping the wrong person will one day become Mr. or Mrs. Right. These types of issue, which should motivate positive change, only seem to bring about more destructive behaviors for certain individuals.

I have also found that things which seem to be positive or harmless can also become barriers to change. I have encountered individuals who have good jobs, good relationships, good health, and live comfortable lives. For this reason they have no plans or desires to make any changes; they feel they are fine just as they are. I do agree that there is absolutely nothing wrong with anyone desiring to live in a comfortable space, but what if there is the potential to gain so much more than what's been settled for?

One individual can be in a bad place with the potential to become good. Another can be in a good place with the potential to become great. But essentially they are both still in the same place if neither of them are attempting to change their lives for the better.

The point I'm making is that the negative or potentially negative outcomes of life do not always prompt people to make changes. No matter how tough life gets, how many mistakes we make, or how many potential pitfalls life may present, "**change**" is not always pushed to the forefront of our thinking. We become too busy, too comfortable, too afraid, too intimidated, too stubborn, even too lazy to take the necessary steps to bring needed or even predestined changes into our lives.

For some reason we have a tendency to believe that life will just change for the better on its own. We believe that one day we'll be rich, one day we'll be drug free, one day we'll find a soul mate, one day we will live in the house on the hill! And while it's great **and necessary** that we believe that our **"one day"** is coming, if I asked what we were doing in our **"present day"** to ensure that our **"one day"** will come, many of us would not have an answer. All because we have just not taken the time to consider the part that we must play in achieving the life that God has promised us.

Taking these things into consideration I was motivated to title this book "Change or Die". Having come to realization that life does not seem to be a strong enough motivator to causes people to make positive - life altering changes, it was laid on my heart by God to present the idea of death as a motivational tool.

Imagine dying having never sought to reach your full potential. Imagine dying having never been able to say that everything you set out to do has been completed or at least attempted. Imagine dying with nothing to leave for your children because you simply lived trying to put food on the table instead of putting a million dollar idea to work. Imagine dying having never made the changes that you told yourself you would make time and time again. Now consider this: what if the longevity of your days are directly connected to the changes that you make? Imagine God making the decision - because you refuse to make changes - your life is now expendable. Imagine God deciding that since you will not change, he now has to make an example out of you to show others the consequences of complacency. I know it's tough to imagine, but I must tell you, if you do not make the necessary changes in your life, the things I have mentioned are realistic possibilities.

The bible warns us **"not to be deceived, because God is not mocked" (Gal 6:7, KJV)**. To "mock" means to taunt or to tease. And I can think of no bigger way to tease God than to present him with hollow words and unused potential. He's placed a gift within each one of us, he has great plans for each one of us, and to watch us go about life without attempting to fully tap into those things is the same as being a tease. God will not allow this.

The scripture goes on to say **"whatever a man sows that shall he also reap"**. Think about this scripture the next time you allow yourself to believe that positive change will just happen on its own. We know that God could change our lives any day and at any time, and he knows that we know this. The danger in knowing is that we have the potential to become reluctant to make changes ourselves - believing that God will just change everything for us **one day**. But this is not so. God says whatever YOU sow into what YOU want is what YOU will reap from what YOU want. Plainly speaking, if we want to see things change there is a part that WE must play and work that WE must do!

This book is designed to enlighten you to the work that must be done in order to see the change that you seek. Along this walk you will be challenged, you will be enlighten, you will be inspired, but most importantly you will be equip to make the necessary changes in your life! Remember this statement: _"where and how you live is usually where and how you die"_. If what is happening or not happening in your life at this very moment is not enough to push you to change, I am hoping that the thought of your life ending as it is today will provide the push that you need! You've got too much to live for to allow a few changes, major or minor, to stand in the way of the life that you deserve and have been promised! The bible says that you will reap what you sow, but it also says **"my God will supply your needs according to HIS riches and glory" (Phil 4:19, KJV)**. That tells me that if I put in the work - if I do my part to bring about the change that I seek, not only will I reap what I sow, but I have the ability to reap according to God's countless and endless resources. God is telling us that if we just do the work, we will receive our due compensation and so much more!

The book of Matthew, chapter 8, tells the story of a disciple who wanted to follow Jesus - but he asked if he could first go and bury his father. Jesus replies by telling the disciple to "follow him (Jesus) now and to let the dead bury the dead". Was Jesus trying to be insensitive to the concerns of this disciple? Not at all; he was simply trying to convey the importance and urgency associate with change. The disciple wanted to linger where he was and deal in death, but Jesus is challenging him to leave his past behind **now** and follow him to a greater life.

Jesus tells the disciple to "let the dead bury the dead". He was telling the disciple to let those who were dead spiritually bury the one who had died naturally. These people were considered dead because they had not or would not peruse changing their lives. They had no desire to achieve God's plan or submit to his will. This way of thinking not only robbed them of living a promised and purposed life, but their lack of change robbed them of even being categorized as "living". This scripture lets us know one very important thing: *you don't have to be dead to be considered dead.*

This Scripture ties directly to the purpose of this book. Not to frighten or condemn you, but to enlighten you to the fact that death is not just a onetime occurrence – it can also become a life style. If you are not pursuing changes that will cause you to live a life of fulfillment and promise, God himself could one day consider you to be dead, even with breath in your lungs and movement in your limbs.

My friend, I don't want that for you. I want you to live the life that you see in your spirit. I want you to be the person that you were born to be and to have all that your potential has the ability to gain for you! In order to get there you are going to have to make changes. It won't be easy, but nothing worth having ever is. The good news is you are not alone. I am right here with you, and most importantly God is in your corner. He's behind you, he's on either side of you, and he's walking this path with you - protecting you as you go. He's even standing at the end of this road, cheering you on to victory, and waiting in anticipation for you to cross the finish line!

There are a lot of changes to be made in your life and even more blessings to be gained in your life. Let's make those changes and get those blessings, together! Here we go!

CHANGE or DIE

PART 1
THE REALIZATION OF CHANGE

Chapter 1

Truth and Transparency with Yourself

Back in the summer of 1938 two men named Bill Wilson and Dr. Bob Smith founded an organization known today as Alcoholics Anonymous. This program is built on 12 core principles or steps that have been proven to outline a course of action for recovery from addiction, compulsion or other behavioral problems. I was always familiar with the 12 step program pertaining to addiction or behavioral problems, but when I read about this recovery system applying also to *compulsion* it brought these steps into a totally new light for me. Many of us have used the word *compulsive* to describe others or maybe even ourselves in certain situations. But I think that we've used the word without fully understanding what it means. Dictionary.com defines *compulsion as a strong, usually irresistible impulse to perform an act, especially one that is irrational or contrary to ones will.* The World English Dictionary defines compulsion as *an inner drive that causes a person to perform actions, often of a trivial and repetitive nature, against his or her own will.* These two definitions vary in their description, but they both have one thing in common - they agree that compulsive behaviors are actions performed by a person against "that persons" **own** will. If you are pursuing change this definition more than likely describes you.

What You Know vs. What You Do

At some point, we all have closed our eyes and been able to see ourselves in a better space. We know what to do and what not to do to cause the things we envision to become reality. But when you examine all of the things you know and then consider all of the things you do - if your *ways* are not in line with your *will* I'm afraid you struggle with compulsiveness.

Let's revisit the definition one more time. *Compulsion is a strong, usually irresistible impulse to perform an act, especially one that is irrational.* What is an *irrational* act? It is one that cannot be explained nor *justified*. In order to achieve change you must ask yourself <u>"can you truly justify your position in life"</u>? You may be able to explain how you've ended up where you are, but the key is your ability to justify the reason. The theological definition for the word "justify" is to *"declare or make righteous in the sight of God"*. If you can look over your life and truly say that God is in favor of all of your actions and decisions; if you can truly say that your place in life is exactly where God would have you to be and all of your behaviors fall in line with his requirements, I congratulate you. There is no need for you to change anything about yourself. You are free to close this book and continue living your perfect life.

My guess is that you are still reading.

The bible says that the righteous are "scarcely "saved (1 Pet 4:18, KJV). It also says that **"the righteous man falls seven times" (Prov 24:16, KVJ)**. Even those who are considered righteous still have changes to make. *In order to change you must first be truthful and transparent concerning the areas of your life that cannot be justified in the sight of God.* It is extremely important to connect God with justification because our since of righteousness and justice has more than likely been negatively impacted by the trials of life.

Later in our reading I will tell you a story involving a woman who commits a terrible act due to a famine that spread through her land. Instead of being humble she seeks justice from her king. She feels that the unfair suffering she endures because of the famine justifies her behavior. Our trials often have the same impact on us. We feel that because we have suffered through things unfairly we are justified in however we choose to react or respond. We are only human, and our flesh has the potential to cause us to respond out of pain and frustration - to pass judgment out of spite or put feelings over forgiveness. But God's righteousness is unwavering and his justification is without malice or bias. His judgment is not clouded, his love is unconditional, and his willingness to forgive is without limits. So taking the theological definition of "justification" into consideration, allow me to ask you a few questions…

- ❖ Can you justify your relationship with God?
- ❖ Can you justify your relationship with your spouse or significant other?
- ❖ Can you justify your relationships with your family and friends?
- ❖ Can you justify your present financial situation?
- ❖ Can you justify the conditions of your living situation?
- ❖ Can you justify the state of your career?
- ❖ Can you justify your habits, behaviors or addictions?

Before you answer, remember, *your justification must be based on rather or not these things are right in the sight of God*. If you have answered "no" to any of these questions, it is time for you to make changes in your life.

Free Time is "Me" Time

Compulsion is as an inner drive that causes a person to perform actions, often of a **trivial and repetitive** nature, against his or her own will. Trivial and repetitive actions are behaviors or activities that are not important but are still being done continuously. I'd like you to consider three things if you will...

- ❖ *First, consider the things that have provoked your need to change.*
- ❖ *Next, consider the amount of time and effort you put into changing those things.*
- ❖ *Last, consider the things you actually put your time and efforts into on a daily basis.*

There are 24 hours in a day. If you work an 8 hour shift and sleep 8 hours through the night, what are you doing with the remaining 8 hours? If you work 5 days a week, what do you do with the other 2 days? How much of that time are you putting into your own dreams? Even if you work more than 8 hours a day, 5 days a week, you still have time away from the responsibilities of life. What are you doing with that time? Most of us will say that we have family obligations or errands to run, and I don't dispute that. I am a husband and father myself, so I understand the importance of dedicating time and attention to the home. But if you are going to change your life you must ask yourself "am I really as busy as I say I am"?

Take all of your responsibilities out of the picture. Now think of how much time and resources you've spent on recreational or leisurely activities such as...

- ❖ Eating out at restaurants
- ❖ Seeing movies, concerts, sporting events, etc;
- ❖ Shopping
- ❖ Parties/Happy Hour
- ❖ Scrolling Social Media and Internet Websites
- ❖ Talking and texting on the phone
- ❖ Watching television
- ❖ Aiding family and friends
- ❖ Sleeping in on Saturday and Sunday

No consider how much time and resources these types of things put back into your life. Don't get me wrong, everyone needs to spoil themselves from time to time. Life is stressful, and if you don't have something to bring yourself enjoyment you will put yourself at risk of having a nervous breakdown. Time away from your responsibilities is your "**free time**" - to do with as you please. As much as you need these types of outlets you still must consider this: ***free time is the only reoccurring time in your life that costs you.*** This is important to remember because most people seem to believe that their obligations and responsibilities provide the barriers to achieving their true purpose in life. This is not true. You earn a living on your job, you earn an education while in school, you fulfill your greatest calling by spending time with your family, and you gain strength and refreshment while sleeping through the night, and taking "power naps" when you need them. The time you spend performing your responsibilities is not your hindrance, but it is what you do with the time "in-between" your responsibilities that determine who and what you really become.

There will come a day when your true purpose will become a reality. It will become so big and successful that it will require a great deal of your time and attention. You will either have a "dream job" or you will be running your own business! Both will require a great deal of your time. But this will only happen if you dedicate your "free time" to that purpose now! *If you truly want to change your life you must take on the mentality that "**free time is me time**"*. Not in the since of treating or indulging yourself, but you must utilize this time to make improvements to yourself.

Again I say "there is nothing wrong with treating yourself from time to time". But if the time you spend spoiling and indulging yourself is more than the time you spend improving yourself, I must tell you that the majority of the things that you do in your free time are repetitively trivial. These things may feel fulfilling while you are doing them, but in the grand scheme of your life they are adding nothing to you.

- ❖ Can you be truthful and transparent enough to admit that you sometimes exhibit irrational behaviors?
- ❖ Can you be truthful and transparent enough to admit that you continuously take part in trivial activities?

If you want to change these irrational and trivial areas of your life you must first be able to admit that they exist. You must also recognize how threatening they can be to the person you are attempting to become! This is tougher than you think, because no matter how irrational or trivial some of your actions have been, odds are you still enjoy doing them! You may hate that you enjoy them but you still enjoy them none the less.

Change vs. Flesh

*Question - Why do we enjoy doing irrational or trivial things? Answer - We are more dedicated to our **flesh** than we are dedicated to our **future**.*

1 Cor 9:26-27 (KJV) - I therefore so run, not as uncertainly; so fight I, not as one that beateth the air: But I keep under my body, and bring it into <u>subjection</u>: lest that by any means, when I have preached to others, I myself should be a castaway.

Being brought under *"subjection"* means to be made or forced to behave as instructed. If your body is doing the instructing, you are always going to be in trouble because the body very seldom craves what it needs; the body general gives more effort to acquiring what it wants. Once the body has acquired a desire for what it wants it can be very difficult to let go of that desire. Your body always wants to do what feels best, the danger is that feelings will deceive you, and eventually destroy you.

Please understand, _as you walk this road to change, you are going to experience a great deal of familiar feelings and desires. Many of them will be contrary to who you are trying to become._ Attempting to change does not guarantee that every negative feeling will immediately dissolve. In fact, there is a good chance those feelings will intensify as your flesh begins to adjust. You must remember that these feelings are not an indication that you are not changing for the better, it is actually proof that you are!

When drug addicts attempt to kick their habit, their bodies go through changes that are called *withdrawals*. Withdrawals are the body's intense reaction to not having what it has been used to receiving. The pains associated with withdrawals are so intense that doctors prescribe a different medication as a means of soothing the discomfort. When change causes you to feel pain, don't panic, just know that the pain is evidence that you are withdrawing from your old life and your positive change is taking effect!

The Benefit of Pain

Change is beneficial, but it is also painful! And unfortunately for us God does not always supply pain killers. Paul validates this in **2 Cor, 12:8 (TLB)**, where he asks God 3 times to ease his pain, but God told him "no". You must understand, *God is not cruel but he uses pain as a tool for long term correction*. His hope is that once your issues have subsided, the thought or memory of the suffering you once had to endure will aid you in not returning to the behaviors of your past.

God also uses pain as a motivational tool for strengthening ones faith. When you have dealt with a pain that medication and worldly pleasures cannot cure, **you will** find your way to God. You will also resolve within yourself that believing in him is the only way to deal with the pain that you feel. The evidence of this is found in verse 9, where God explains to Paul *"I am with you; that is all you need. My power shows up best in weak people"*! Paul then says *"Now I am glad to boast about how weak I am; I am glad to be a living demonstration of Christ's power, instead of showing off my own power and abilities"*. Paul understood what you must understand during this process: <u>God leaves urges in our flesh, so that every time we resist an urge we will know that there is something greater than that urge on the inside of us</u>!

When it comes to your fleshly issue, your problem is not that you like it, the problem is that you do it! You may never be able to change what you like, but your task now is only to change what you do. The easiest thing for you would be for God to just take the desire away, but <u>change does not come easy, even when God is involved</u>. If you want to change my friend, you must let go of the notion that God is going to just take away your urges, cravings and desires. Paul's experience shows us that this is not a guarantee. God is not going to take away everything because he wants you to have victory over your issues, not just to avoid them.

He wants you to be a champion of change, not just a recipient of mercy.

Compulsiveness Leads To Change

A vital piece to changing is to admit that you have ways that are compulsive. You must be able to recognize irrational behavior, identify trivial activities, and the repetitive ways these things continue to impact your life. You must also remember that the most important aspect of the compulsiveness is that it causes you to do things against your own will. The best way to remedy this is to replace your will with the will of God. You have to come to the same conclusion as Jesus Christ after praying in the garden of Gethsemane. Jesus asked the Father to take away the painful road that lied ahead for him. This request was not granted. So Jesus tells the Father what you must say to him also, **"not my will, but yours be done" (Lk 22:42, NASB)**.

God needs you to be someone who understands who you are and what you are involved in. You must understand that the best place you could be is a place where you cannot achieve your change on your own, and you are now giving God the stage to step in and perform a great miracle in your life!

Challenged to Change

I challenge you stop reading for just a few seconds. Have a conversation with God. Admit to him that you are absolutely nothing without him! Admit to him that your power is insufficient and you need a power greater than your own. Paul described it as "The Power of Christ"! Before you proceed to the next chapter I urge you to pray for that same power! Pray until you feel stronger, pray until you feel invigorated, pray until you feel powerful, and then come back and continue this conversation with me in the next chapter.

Chapter 2

Truth and Transparency with People

On your journey to change please remember this scripture...

1 Sam 16:7 (HCSB) - "But the LORD said to Samuel, "Do not look at his appearance or his stature, because I have rejected him. Man does not see what the LORD sees, for man sees what is visible, but the LORD sees the heart."

This scripture is one of many which confirm that God deals in transparency. Not mere words, feelings, thoughts or opinions. When it comes to the need for change God wants you to be real with yourself and real with him.

The scripture also informs us that man will judge you from the outside, which means that people can only judge you by what you show them. This is actually an advantage for you. While it is necessary to be real with yourself and God, it is also sometimes necessary to project something different for the people around you. I am not advising you to lie, but in order to make changes you must find a way to conceal your issues without being dishonest about them. You must learn how to wear your regal robe on the outside and your sackcloth underneath (I'll provide more detail for this later in our reading).

The Opinions of Others

When you are changing, you cannot freely expose your issues to everyone. You must remember that people are not always happy for you, especially when it looks to them as if you are maturing to a place that they cannot relate to. The bible instructs us to **"lay aside every weight and sin that does so easily beset us"**. Prior to that, in the same verse it says that **"we are compassed about with so great a cloud of witnesses" (Heb 12:1, KJV)**. This means that while you are attempting to make changes there will be a number of onlookers. People will be watching and waiting to give their opinion concerning your new way of life.

Some will try to talk you out of changing; they will attempt to make you feel as if you can't change. They will tell you that it's too late for you, you've been doing what you've been doing for too long and time has passed you by. Never allow yourself to believe this! Abraham was 100 years, and his wife Sarah was 90 years old when their first child Isaac was born. The bible says that Abraham **"not being weak in faith, did not consider his own body, already dead (since he was about a hundred years old), and the deadness of Sarah's womb. He did not waver at the promise of God through unbelief, but was strengthened in faith, giving glory to God, and being fully convinced that what He (God) had promised He (God) was also able to perform" (Rom 4:19, NKJV)**.

Why would God allow them to conceive and birth a child so far beyond child bearing age? *God had to fulfill his promise to them before they died*! You must understand that God's promises do not expire, even when it looks like your opportunities are slipping away from you. You are never too old to change and change is not overrated. As long as there is breathe in your body and a promise on your life, change still applies to you and will work for you. Don't ever allow anyone to convince you otherwise!

Beware of Nice People

People will attempt to convince you that you are fine the way you are; but you must remember that you know better! _Nothing makes giving up on change easier than being close to someone who won't look down on you for giving up._ People who encourage you to quit or try to convince that you do not need to change are not always negative naysayers.

You will encounter people who are genuinely worried about you. They may believe that the change you seek is too much for you to handle, and they just don't want you to be hurt or embarrassed - attempting to do something they feel is out of your reach. You will have people who will speak negatively of your change simply because they like you or love you the way that you are. They may fear the impact that your change will have on your relationship with them. And then of course, you will encounter people who just cannot see the benefit in what you are trying to do or who you are trying to become. They will mean you no harm; they will just feel and express that your time would be better served doing other things. This is why I warn you to not only be leery of naysayers but to also be careful of *nice people*.

Nice people are not always honest. They don't want to hurt your feelings and they would prefer to avoid confrontation. They will say negative things in a nice manner – making you comfortable as they cut into you. They will also say nice things to make you feel good instead of being painfully honest when you need it most. Don't get me wrong - it is always better to be nice and to have nice people around you, but when you are attempting to change the last thing you need is someone who will constantly praise your qualities while overlooking your deficiencies. *You need someone that will tell you the truth without using the truth as a weapon*.

This works both ways. If you are connected to a person that only seems to be pleased with pointing out your issues, I would advise you to alter or terminate your relationship with that person immediately. They may be honest but because they only notice or highlight your negatives they will fall short in providing you the encouragement you will need to continue to pursue your change.

People who only praise you will never help you grow, and people who only criticize you will stunt your growth. In order to change you need a healthy balance of constructive criticism and congratulations, and you must surround yourself with people that provide that balance.

Beware of People with Similar Struggles

When concealing your issues you must also remember the old saying, "birds of a feather flock together"! People seem to gravitate to other people who have their same struggle - sometimes even without knowing. When they actually do find out that the two of you are experiencing the same issue they will become your friend and attempt to change with you. This may seem noble or encouraging but even this can be dangerous. You must remember: *anyone who has your struggles also has your weaknesses, and how can they help you if they cannot help themselves?*

The bible says that **every man is to work out his own salvation, with fear and trembling** (Phil 2:12, KVJ). *You have to be so intent on changing that you are afraid to allow the wrong person to get too close.* Two people who don't know how to swim will both drown in deep waters. Learn to surround yourself with life guards while you are swimming toward your change.

The Expectations of People

Some people will use your attempt to change against you. Once they find out you do not like or are attempting to change a certain thing about yourself they will use that thing to attempt to control you. *A person who is changing needs the freedom to make mistakes without having to re-start the process each time they drop the ball.* When people know that you are trying to change they will sometimes try to hold you to it - no matter what. Even if they have not made the changes that you are attempting to make, they will still look at you and expect you to be different. If what they see does not line up with you said they will hold it over your head.

Others will provoke you and manipulate you - just because they know that you promised to stop doing a certain negative thing. They will do things to draw that negativity out of you and then shame you for not sticking to who you said you where becoming. They will offer you a cigarette and then shame you for smoking it. They will start an argument with you and then shame you for losing your temper. They will seduce you and then shame you for giving in to temptation. Some people are just bitter toward the idea of change because they have no drive or power to change their own lives. They expect you to fail because they've failed, and they will do anything they can to prove that your attempt to change in useless. *Quitters not only quit on themselves, but they encourage quitting in others.* Along this road to change I warn you to be careful not to become a victim to the expectations of people.

Allow me to share this with you. I became a Pastor in 2012. Earlier in that same year I took a leadership position for a large corporation. I have always been a "mild mannered" individual. As a leader I do my best to maintain my demeanor, but when the situation calls I can become very aggressive, vocal and stern in my expectations. When I started with the company the people seem to be accepting of my personality, but after they found out I was a pastor their expectations became very different. They began to expect me to always be kind and gentle no matter the situation - never to raise my voice or become angry, and to always smile and be cordial to everyone that I met. They expected me to mingle and be social; to ask them about their outside lives and understand their personal struggles, even when those things were impacting their ability to properly perform their duties on the job. I tried to fit their perception, but whenever I fell short some would murmur, and others would say to my face "how are you going to be a Pastor acting the way that you do"! Even on the job the people did not want to see "Devaughn Kelly – Supervisor" they wanted to see "Devaughn Kelly – Senior Pastor".

What they would not accept or refused to understand was that even though I am a Pastor I was still an employee. I still had a job to do and I while at work I needed to perform my duties. They also did not seem to understand that life was difficult at times for me the same as it was for everyone else. I would have my breaking points, my tough days, and at that time, I was a new Pastor. I had only recently changed my life to walk in my calling and I was still going through the transition process.

My points were valid but the critics could not care less. The minute you pronounce that you are different or trying to become different, people expect to see what **they feel** you should be. If you do not live up to their expectations they will attempt to hold you accountable, even when they have no authority to do so.

Be Careful What You Say to People

Changing my life to become a Pastor was something that I could not conceal, but I have a feeling the things that you need to change do not require the same visibility. If you have issues with your flesh, drugs, smoking, lying, relationships, money, etc; people don't have to know. You **will not** be able to keep your struggles from everyone no matter how hard you try, but it is important that you are very selective with whom you reveal your vulnerabilities to. *Remember: changes must not only be made but they must also be protected.*

Am I asking you never to testify? Absolutely not. What I am saying is that you must know when and with whom to share your testimony. *While you are walking through the process of change your first priority must be to strengthen yourself first. You are no good to others if you are no good to yourself*. In order to do this you must conceal your weaknesses until they are no longer weaknesses. Some conversations are meant for you to testify, others are meant for you to be tested; you must be able to identify one from the other. If you cannot determine when to share and when to conceal, the best thing to do is to conceal. You can always conceal a thing, but once you share it you can never take it back. Once it leaves your mouth it cannot be unsaid, and how those words come back to you cannot be dictated.

Jeremiah, the writer of **Lamentation chapter 3, verse 26 says "a men should both hope and quietly wait on the salvation of the Lord" (KJV).** Prior to saying this he had spent time verbally expressing his pain and displeasure with what God had allowed him to go through. He finally comes to the realization that God has kept him through it all! In his reflection he realizes that he should have died in his struggle, but due to God's mercy he is not consumed. This revelation leads him to declare that he will stop talking about what he's going through openly. He decides that he would stop lamenting, broadcasting, and posting about things that he needs changed. In order to change you have to take on the mindset of Jeremiah; you have to believe that God will not allow what you're dealing with to linger forever. So until those things have changed you will not freely or recklessly expose them to people any longer.

Choose the Right People

The bible tells us in 1 Samuel that man will see and believe what you show them, so while you are changing don't show them anything that could cause them to hinder your progress. Don't get me wrong, it is perfectly fine to find someone to confide in, but that person should be someone who you trust not to pull you backwards. You should choose only one or two…maybe three people to confide in at the most. Family members cannot be exempt from this process of elimination. Everybody is related to somebody - we can't choose our relatives, but we must make the proper choices concerning them. If they are not trust worthy do not confide in them...period. Find just a few people that you know you can trust.

Knowing who to keep close and who to distance yourself from is not going to be easy. For some of us it is the people that are closest to us that present the biggest problem. For others, simply keeping quiet is going to be an issue. Talking is how we sometimes deal with our problems. It is our method of therapy. It is our way of lightening our mental load. We tell people our struggles hoping they will comfort us, encourage us, or help to point us in the right direction. I totally understand this way of thinking and the difficulty that change in this area will present. But this is what change is all about; making difficult decisions and adjustments when it comes to the people in our lives.

Challenged to Change

I challenge you yet again to put down this book and have another conversation with God. Ask him to give you wisdom concerning people. It is important that you make a habit of asking the Lord to show you who you need to keep close and who you need to let go of? A large factor in your ability to change is how you interact with people; only God knows those who mean you well and those who will have a negative impact on your life. You are only human and you will also judge people by what they show you. For this reason you will not always be able to determine the sheep from the wolves. If you want to keep the right people close and the wrong people at arm's length you are going to have to consult the Lord continuously. I challenge you to start this conversation now. Talk to the Lord about the peopled in your life and then come back and talk to me in chapter 3.

Chapter 3

Truth and Transparency with God

Another scripture to remember is…

Psalm 139:1 - "You have searched me, Lord, and you know me (NIV)"

<u>People see what you show them but God sees what you conceal. God sees what you cover up. God sees what you try to ignore</u>. As I said before God deals in truth and transparency, and he only reacts positively to the same,

"truth and transparency". In the Old Testament the Lord watched the Israelites, his people, sin and become captives continuously. Through his grace and mercy he always delivered them but only after they or someone cried out to him on their behalf. The point I am making is that somebody had to be honest and transparent before God would move. Even in the New Testament, Jesus would talk to people before or after healing them. He would ask their back story, why they wanted to be healed, or if they wanted to be healed. He would also sometimes inform them of what they must do to remain healed. These things had to be discussed, because if change was to take place truth and transparency had to be in mix.

Psalms 139:1 says that God knows us because he searches us. He doesn't take our word for it, he doesn't go along with the façade that we attempt to project, he goes beyond our flesh, our word, and even our feelings, and he sees the truth. So if God can see it what's the point in trying to hide it from him?

<u>Trying to hide your issues from God is not only useless but it prolongs your process of change.</u> God holds time in his

hands; he created it and he controls it. For this reason God can wait forever for you to be honest and transparent. Unfortunately you don't have the same convinces. While God holds and controls time, day by day you are losing time and the opportunities it presents; so you may as well get this out of the way right now!

Challenged to Change

I challenge you to stop reading for a few moments, drop down on your knees and have a transparent conversation with God. Tell him who you are, what you are, and what you've done. Hold back nothing - be totally honest and open, and then repent for everything! Truly repent! How do you know when repentance is true? If you plan to continue to do what you've been doing after you've repented then you have not truly repented. I warn you, you may not be immediately able to get out of what you've gotten yourself into. But if you repent, with a made up mind and honest intentions, then your repentance is true and your deliverance is imminent.

This chapter is extremely short for a very specific reason. Your need to converse with God concerning **you** far outweighs my need to converse with you. Lack of honesty and repentance with God will put everything you attempt to change in jeopardy. *Your connection with God has to be through relationship, not just dependency*. He's not your genie in a bottle, your public official, or your hired hand...he is your God! You're Savior, your Father and your Friend! As such you must build a relationship with him based on honesty.

The truth hurts, but I have learned that hurting and healing go hand in hand. I challenge you to talk to the Lord until it hurts. The things that come out of your mouth may cause you to cry, scream, or even experience a break down, but that's OK. After all, how can you be fixed if you can't admit that you are broken? Before you read any longer, take a few minutes, take a few hours if you need to, and allow yourself to be broken before the Lord. Once you've done that come back and we will move on to chapter 4.

Chapter 4

You Will Never Be Ready

Ready vs. Willing

Let's take a look at Romans chapter 7 in the Living Bible...

In verse 15 Paul declares "I don't understand myself at all, for I really want to do what is right, but I can't"!

One of the biggest reasons for our struggles is that we often feel that we can fix them on our own. When resisting the need to change, one of the most often used excuses is "I'm not ready". Many of us *consciously* live beneath our purpose in life, holding on to the thinking that **"one day"** we will just wake up a changed person. We genuinely feel that **"one day"** we will give our lives over to a better plan and a higher purpose, but only when we are **"ready"**.

What we don't understand, and what I always try to explain, is that *change is about being willing, not being ready. The truth is you will **never** truly be ready to change. You will say that you are, you will think that you are, but how can you truly be ready when you don't know what's coming?* How can you determine when you will be ready when you have no control over time, nor the elements that time may bring. You have no clue when you are going to die. You have no clue if a terrible accident will paralyze your thinking or mobility. You have no clue if a loved one will be hurt or taken away. Since you have no control over what may happen next how can you know when to be ready?

I knew of a man who was assumed to be righteous, but behind closed doors he had extramarital affairs with several women and had children out of wedlock. He knew that his lifestyle was not in line with his beliefs but he went years doing the same thing. Eventually he became mentally ill. He acquired Alzheimer's disease and could no longer comprehend. Unfortunately, his Alzheimer's set in before he took steps to change his life. He is still living but cannot change nor repent for the things that he has done because his mental capacity has been taken from him. I'm sure he said many times "I'll change when I'm ready", but he could never have imagined he would be alive and still not have the ability to make things right.

In order to change, you have to throw this notion of **"being ready"** out off the window. You have to take on the mindset that you will never be ready. You are never going to stop this on your own. You are always going to find a reason to go back to what you need to leave behind. You **must** take on this mentality immediately. Why? Because *"not being ready"* will always be your *"get out of change free"* card! As long as you can say it and believe it, you will always utilize it when changing gets tough.

So how can you truly change if you are not ready to do so? Fortunately for us, being ready to change is not a requirement. The bible says *"if there is first a willing mind, it is accepted according to what one has, and not according to what he does not have"* **(2 Cor 8:12, NKJV)**. <u>When it comes to change, you must act on your **willingness**, not your **readiness**</u>.

Willingness is a Requirement

A perfect example of what I'm saying is the conversion of the apostle Paul in Acts chapter 9. On the road to Damascus - on his way to persecute Christians, Paul (who was then named Saul) is encountered by Jesus Christ himself. Jesus challenges Paul to change his life right then and there. Paul had no intention when he woke up that morning that he would be giving his life to Jesus later that same day; he had not expressed even an interest in doing so. But when Jesus encountered him on that road he was *willing* to change. Willingness surpasses readiness, simply because it requires nothing but a yes. It only requires that you show up and be open to participate.

Change or Die

As a pastor I am constantly inviting people to church! One of the many reasons I hear for why people cannot come is "they have nothing to wear". Yes, even in this day of generation x and millennial pastors who preach Sunday morning messages wearing tee shirts and blue jeans, there are still people who claim that they cannot come to church because they don't have a nice enough suit or dress. It's not a bad thing to want to be presentable and formal for church, the problem is that they are missing the purpose of what the church is supposed to do for them. It's not about how you walk in but it's all about what you take with you when you leave. In the bible people came to Jesus just as they were. I've never read a scripture that says that someone put on their best clothes just to speak with Jesus. As a matter of fact, the only story that comes close is the story of Jesus and the rich young ruler.

The book of Mark tells of an instance where a rich young ruler came to Jesus asking what he must do to inherit eternal life. Jesus told him that he must sell all of his possessions and give them to the poor. Upon hearing this, the ruler became very sad and walks away from Jesus. The bible says that this young ruler had kept all of the commandments from his youth. Because of this I believe that he felt he was *ready* for whatever Jesus asked him to do. Sadly he wasn't, and it caused him to walk away from the eternal life he desired to gain. Jesus knew about this young man keeping the commandments, he also knew that because of this, the man thought that he was ready for the next step, but Jesus wasn't looking for readiness he was looking for willingness. The clothes and the money meant nothing to Jesus; his main concern was this young man gaining what had been set aside for him by God. In order to obtain this new life the man needed to be willing to separate from his possessions, even if he wasn't ready.

Uncomfortable Instructions

<u>*Change is going to come with instructions that will make you uncomfortable*</u>. You are going to be required to do things that you are simply not ready to do. You are not always going to like these instructions. You are not always going to understand them. These instructions may make absolutely no since to you at all; but they must be followed. Why would Jesus ask that man to sell all of his possessions? He worked for them, earned them, or inherited them;

however he received them they belonged to him. Jesus gave no explanation, no reason why, he just said to do it. What the man was told was that after he sold and gave away his possessions he was to come back and follow. If Jesus is the one giving the instructions then Jesus has to be the one to cover those who follow the instructions. Jesus was asking the man to be wiling…not ready…to empty himself of everything he had built his confidence in and to follow him to the new life that he seeks. Unfortunately the young ruler was not willing to comply.

My friend, if you want change you can't be like this rich young rule, or the individual who will only come to church if they can come through the doors looking like a million bucks. <u>You **cannot** be willing to pursue change "on your terms only"</u>. Change means letting go of anything that keeps you from you purpose. You must *let go* of the belief that you cannot *let go*!

<u>When you say that you want to change, **you will** be tested. God's most common way of testing is by making parts of the process extremely uncomfortable for you</u>. You must remember and believe that he is not trying to make you

give up, but he's trying to answer two very important questions concerning your commitment...

- ❖ How serious are you about achieving the change you seek?
- ❖ How serious are you about keeping the change once you achieve it?

The enemy is going to attack you at every opportunity. He will attempt to steal, contaminate, pervert or belittle everything you gain from this process of change. <u>*If you cannot hold on when God is testing you then you will surely fail when the enemy is attacking you*</u>.

I once preached a message called "Don't Get Tired of Your Fatigue". The word *"fatigue"* means to be tired, worn out or exhausted. It is also used to describe the uniforms worn by soldiers on the field of battle. When you are attempting to change you are going to wear a great deal of fatigue. But you must remember your fatigue identifies you - not just as being a tired individual, but also as a soldier - fighting to **WIN** a battle! For that reason you cannot take it off and you cannot allow it to cause you to quit! Your "change" is going to present you with requirements that are going to almost zap your mental and physical strength, but you must wear your fatigue and continue to fight until you win!

Challenged to Change

I challenge you once more to lay down this book and do a self examination. In order to achieve your change you are going to have to be willing to face your issues head on. You are going to have to be willing to drop everything if you must and move toward your destiny. Most importantly, you are going to have to be willing to do everything the Lord tells you to do, even if you do not understand or agree. I challenge you to give a true examination of your willingness to change; and if you find that you are not willing I ask that you would pray. Ask God to give you a willing heart. Ask him to give you the mind and the strength to follow him faithfully without hesitation. Talk to yourself concerning your willingness. Talk to the Lord concerning your willingness. And then join me in chapter 5.

Chapter 5

If You Can Change Why Haven't You?

Admit What You Can't Do

We began the last chapter speaking about Romans chapter 7, let's go back and speak more about this scripture.

In verse 21 Paul continues on to say "it seems to be a fact of life that when I want to do what is right, I inevitably do what is wrong. I love to do God's will so far as my new nature is concerned but there is something else deep within me, in my lower nature, that is at war with my mind and wins the fight and makes me a slave to the sin that is still within me. In my mind I want to be God's willing servant, but instead I find myself still enslaved to sin. So you see how it is: my new life tells me to do right, but the old nature that is still inside me loves to sin. Oh, what a terrible predicament I'm in! Who will free me from my slavery to this deadly lower nature (Rom 7:21-24, TLB)"?

Like Paul, can you be real enough to look over your life and say "Oh what terrible predicament I'm in"!

- ❖ I'm out of control.
- ❖ I just can't get it right.
- ❖ I say that I'm not going to a certain place but I constantly find myself returning.
- ❖ I say that I will control my tongue and then someone provokes me to speak ill.

- ❖ I am determined to be better with money and then an unexpected disaster strikes.
- ❖ I want to do "good", but good always seems to conjure up the presence of evil!

Just for a few moments I need to take you back to the beginning of this reading. We started off talking about Alcoholic Anonymous and their 12 step program. Maybe you're not familiar with the actually steps so allow me to share the first one with you: "*we admitted **we were powerless** over alcohol and that our lives had become unmanageable*". In the first chapter we talked to God about our problems, but now we must go further and admit that we are powerless to change them on our own.

At first your admission may make you feel a bit embarrassed, but you have nothing to feel embarrassed about. <u>If *you cannot do a certain thing, acting as if you can is not going to make you better at it. You will only cause more stress, worry and problems piling up in your present which will come back to haunt you in your future*</u>. The beauty in admitting what you cannot do is that it lifts the burden off of your shoulders. If you can't do it, and you admit that you can't do it, eventually the expectation will be lifted and with it the stress. When you admit to God that you are not able to handle a situation, that thing now becomes God's to fix. And who better to fix a problem than the one who already knows the outcome. But here is what you must understand: admitting to something that you cannot do, and being relieved of the expectations associated with it, does not mean that you get to live the rest of your life doing nothing. Quite the contrary; <u>*once you are relieved of the* **"cant do's"** *in your life, it provides even more time to focus on the things that you* **"can do"**</u>.

As I am writing this I am 3 days away from starting a new position on my job and I am very excited! The twister is that the position I am starting is actually a demotion from the position I currently hold. Why would I be excited about a demotion? Because I have come to realize I am not suited to continue operating in my present position? I have interests outside of the work place, and the time that I have spent in this position has shown me that if I want to succeed I must show a dedication that I am just not able, nor interested in giving. It's not that I am lazy or not driven; but my present position intrudes heavily on my life outside of work, which in turn makes it more difficult to pursue my true passions – ministry, media and motivating others! I feel that my present position provides more barriers to being who I am destined to be, while the new position allows me to earn a living and pursue my passions with very little distraction. *In order to gain the ability to pursue after the things that I really want to do in life I had to admit that I could not continue to do the things that I am presently doing*; and my friend, it is time for you to admit the same.

When we admit to things that we cannot do we normally consider things that are sinful or hazardous, but this time around I'd like for you to look at things that you do throughout the course of your day which add no value to your present or your future. Those are things that you must admit that you can no longer do. *You must be able to admit to yourself that you have a tendency to devote time to activities that give nothing back to your dreams, plans, and goals, and you simply don't have that time to dedicate to those things anymore.*

The Gaps of Life

<u>If you want to change you have to structure your life around the things that you are truly destined to be!</u> This will not be easy because there are things in life that you simply **must** do. However, a person who wants change understands that they may have to work in what I call "***the gaps of life***". These are the spaces that your day to day life allows before, after and in between the things that must be done. These gaps would be…

- ❖ Your break and lunch time at work.
- ❖ Slow days at work were your assignments are finished before the end of your working day.
- ❖ The late hours of the night or the wee hours of the morning while the world is still asleep.
- ❖ During the baby's nap time or while the kids are at school.
- ❖ During long holidays where you get a few extra days off of work.
- ❖ Taking paid vacations and staying home to work your plan instead of traveling.

❖ On the weekends, while the world is out enjoying life and having a ball.

Change does not happen on a 9 to 5 schedule - it simply cannot. Change takes sacrificing your time and doing things that are contrary to the things that you would normally do...*that is why it's called "change".*

Give Thanks for Change before the Change Happens

Getting back to our scripture in Romans chapter 7, Paul says "Oh, what a terrible predicament I'm in! Who will free me from my slavery to this deadly lower nature"? But then in the last sentence, after laying all of his issues on the table, he says "Thank God, it has already been done"!

Paul is praising God for a change that he's still looking forward to. He does not wait until the change comes but he begins to give praise and declare that the change has already taken place in his life.

Allow me to share a testimony with you. I used to be an over the road truck driver. My career only last a whopping

4 months, but I did it none the less. I drove to places that were very far from my home and family in Detroit. With the exception of South Dakota I drove a 32 foot tractor trailer through every state in the Midwest and West Coast. During the first few weeks I drove with a partner, but once I passed my driver's test they gave me my own truck. That was probably the loneliest time in my life.

Before working as a truck driver I was a retail manger and I hated it. I would work nights, weekends, holidays, and long hours - sometimes 10 to 12 hours a day as a salaried employee. Yes, that means no over time! I don't think I ever made more than $35,000.00 a year in retail management. All of those hours and sacrifices just to bring home money that never seemed to be enough. On Saturday afternoons when my family was going out to enjoy the weekend I'd be on my way to work. I felt that I was missing so much of my oldest son's development because I always had to work. At a certain point I became fed up and decided to pursue a career in truck driving.

I know it doesn't sound very wise to go over the road and leave my family completely instead of working nights and weekends and still being able to see them every day. But I figured I'd hit the road for a few months and then I'd have enough experience to come home and get a local job that would pay much more and have me home evenings and weekends. Man was I wrong about that! But I had a passion for "change", so I had to at least "pursue the possibility". I started my career in November, and it seemed as though every route took me out west, where there seems to be nothing but mountains, snow and ice. It was lonely, and many days terrifying. I was thousands of miles from home in the middle of nowhere with no one to talk to. My wife and I talked over the phone but it wasn't the same. I had to sleep in the truck, wash my body and brush my teeth in public rest rooms, and pay for every meal - nothing but fast food and junk food. It was lonely and scary.

You may as well hear it and accept it now; _change will sometimes be lonely and scary._ You are not going to always have someone to talk to. You are not always going to be able to rest comfortably. You are not always going to have peace of mind. You are not always going to be in familiar places. But you must continue to move through it and believe that it will all work together for your good! I didn't quit truck driving, truck driving quit me! They fired me, and then blackballed me due to two accidents I had out there on the road. Thank God nobody was hurt or killed. They were just a few parking lot bumps, but they were accidents none the less; and bad enough to end my truck driving career…thank God!

The point of this story is this, while I was out there, pursuing change, it got tough, it got lonely and it got scary. The only thing that kept me through it was to take on the mindset of Paul. I would continue to tell myself that I was already home. I would be in California declaring "this time in my life had already passed and I am already home". New Mexico declaring "this time has passed, I'm not even here, I'm living in my memory, I'm already home"! Black icy mountains in Montana, Colorado and Washington State declaring, WITH MY MOUTH, "this time has already passed, I've lived through it, I've overcome it and it's already finished"! I've driven in conditions that could have killed me, but I believe that I made it through because I spoke as Paul did. In the mist of my situation "Thank God, it has already been done"! *If you want to experience change, you are going to have to speak as if change has already taken place. You must progress from asking God to do it and began to thank him for doing it already! You cannot wait until it's done, you must declare it now!*

Challenged to Change

We are moving to the second division of this book, but before we go there, I challenge you, as you are in the process of change to give God thanks as if your change has already come! Put your praise in front of your blessing! God is a God of order, and if you think about it "thanks for a gift without receiving a gift is out of order"! So as you praise God for your change, the only way for him to put your life in order is to give you what you've already thanked him for! I challenge you yet again, do not turn another page in this book until you thank God for the change that you don't have yet. Thank him as if you've already receive it! Take some time and do this now! I'll catch up with you in part 2!

CHANGE or DIE
PART 2
THE STRESS OF CHANGE

Chapter 6

Stressed Equals Blessed!

It is a fact that stress affects us all. The Stress Management Health Center, found on the WebMD website explains that *"we may notice symptoms of stress when disciplining our kids, during busy times at work, when managing our finances, or when coping with a challenging relationship, among other things. Stress is everywhere. And while a little stress is OK...because some stress is actually beneficial -- too much stress can wear you down and make you sick, both mentally and physically*". There is more for us to highlight from this article but before I move forward allow me to highlight a portion that caught my attention. This article tells us that a little stress is not only OK, but it is actually "**beneficial**". I must admit that upon reading this I was very confused as to how stress could be a benefit. I was so confused that I began to review the symptoms of stress, just to see if I could find any that would validate this claim. Of the 26 symptoms of stress posted on this same web site I found that there is a cognitive symptom of stress that rather we've noticed or not, has in fact provided a benefit to us. That is the symptom of "constant worry".

Yes I will say it again just so we're clear, God revealed to me so that I may in turn reveal to you that **"constant worry" is a benefit to stress**. I know that it may be a bit tough to believe but consider this: *your constant worry has indeed been a benefit, because the only time you really pray about something is when you're really worried about something*. I'm not talking about the simple prayers that we say over our food or the thanks that we give and the requests that we make as we are running out of the door to work in the morning. I'm talking about real prayer: ***on your***

knees, in your private space, no interruptions, no time limits, no fancy routine, loud, sincere, desperate for an immediate answer type of prayer! If you think about it I'm sure you would agree, you are more prone to engage God with real prayer when you are dealing with real worries.

Conditional Communication

Depending on state of our lives, our speaking relationship with God has the potential to become very conditional. In my experiences as a pastor I have discovered a few things that cause conditions to be a factor when it comes to our interaction with God...

- ❖ **Relationship Status** – Single people and people in struggling relationships have a tendency to seek the Lord with more passion. We all have a natural yarning for attention and companionship; when there is not another person to fill that void we cling harder to God. Once a significant other enters the picture things have a strong potential to change. Unless both parties are equally interested in having a relationship with God, the one who is more committed to God is often faced with the need to choose. Unfortunately, God is not always the choice.

- ❖ **Financial Situation** – Most people seem to be less committed to God when their finances are in order. We all see God as a "supplier of needs". Once God supplies those needs we have a tendency to become careless with our communication. Either we speak to God once we've done what we like with our resources or we don't speak with him until our resources have been depleted.

- ❖ **Health and Wellbeing** - I've seen and experienced this personally. When we are battling illnesses, especially those that are either not easily cured or require surgery, we call and depend on God to heal. Wellbeing can be categorized in many ways. Legal trouble, employment issues, threats from other individuals, etc. When we are dealing with any issue that threatens our lives in any way we seek God for protection and security. But when God provides for us we go back to living the same as we did before.

We've all been guilty of conditional communication with God at some point in our lives. When things are going well we fail to give God any extended portions of our time and attention. We will give him our Sunday mornings, and maybe an hour or two during the week, and nothing more. But the second we experience the type of problems that people won't fix, money can't fix, and doctors can't cure we look for God to come through for us. We pray more, we go to church more; we try to become closer to our spiritual leaders. All of these things are fine, unless they are conditional.

Conditional communicators often have **"faith"** but they lack **"faithfulness"**. There is a difference. Faith tells God "I know that your there, I know that you care, and I can depend on you to come through **for me**". Faithfulness says to God "rather you do what I ask or not, I will stick by you, serve you and always come through **for you**"! Faith can be conditional but faithfulness supersedes conditions. Some people only have faith in what they want to receive from God, but faithfulness is shown when you are not receiving everything you want but you are still showing commitment to God.

Conditional Blessings

God is faithful to us. And he shows us; not just by giving us blessings, but because he blesses us even when he knows that we are not going to change after we receive the blessing. I call these "conditional blessings"; when God blesses you regardless of the condition of your life. And let me warn you, if you are receiving conditional blessings this only means that you are being blessed by God's grace. What would be the problem with that you ask? God tells **Paul in 2 Cor 12:9 (KJV) "my grace is sufficient"**! The word sufficient means "just enough". Sufficient will never indicate overflow or abundance; it will always mean "just enough".

In order to receive change you are going to have to take on the mindset that "just enough" will not do. You have to develop a way of thinking and commit to a way living that strives to receive more than just the grace of God! Don't get me wrong, **grace is a wonderful thing** and I thank God for it every day! But think about this: when you receive a bill and the company gives you a grace period, they are really only giving you additional time to handle the payment before they release the penalty.

God's grace works the same way. It does not eliminate penalty, it only gives you more time to handle the issue before the penalty is required! _Grace is necessary, but you must remember that grace comes with a condition_. The condition is that it is "sufficient" and not "endless". Grace is totally God's preference and has the potential to run out at God's discretion. Grace merely provides time and distance between you and the penalties you may have to pay for the life you are presently living. God has given you grace! But you must use this grace to make the necessary changes, so that the penalty will have no impact on your life once your grace period has ended.

From Conditional to Constant

Stress comes from constant worry. The benefit of constant worry is that it should keep you in constant communication with God. You may be in a place in life were you are tired of the things you constantly have to deal with. God sent me to tell you that those things are necessary, because they bring you closer to him! Constant worry is meant to cause you to talk to God about your life, consider him before you act and include him in your processes.

We thank God for hearing us and keeping us in times of stress, but if you want the stress to change, you must change your interaction with God. You cannot reduce him to a mere stress reliever; nothing more than a spiritual aspirin only to be pulled out and consumed when you need to be relieved from pain. You must be consistent with God! *God must be given the same attention when times are good as you would give him when you are faced with the trials of life*. Remember: **it is in him that YOU live, YOU move and have YOUR being (Acts 17:28, KJV)**, not the other way around. God is sovereign, God is omnipresent, God is the creator; it was his **decision** to send his son to the cross to die for our sins, not his **obligation**.

Remember the people of Israel that I referenced a few chapters ago? If you read in the book of Judges you will see that they followed the same cycle. They would be blessed, and in their blessing they would become comfortable. Once they became comfortable they would ignore God in favor of the people who occupied their land with them - people whom God would warn them to stay away from. Before long they would start to follow the customs of their neighbors, abandoning their God to serve other gods. Not long after their treason the Lord would allow their neighbors to oppress them. Once they were oppressed they would remember God again and call out to him for salvation. But once they received salvation they would repeat the cycle again. Some of us live following this same cycle. When life is up we put God down, but when we go down we lift God up. *If you want your life to change, this cycle must change. God has to know that he is always the God of your life and you will put nothing before him*. Not friends, not family, not money, not your career; not even your hopes, dreams and aspirations. God must be at the forefront of it all.

We are all human, and sometimes we become so caught up in trying to *"make it"* that we neglect God inadvertently. We don't mean to ignore him or to put him second in our lives, we simply become so involved in our surroundings and responsibilities that our relationship with him falls by the wayside. Remember this: God *is intentional. Everything he has for you is tailor made for you. Because of this you have to be intentional when it comes to your treatment of him.* You have to intentionally plan to time to spend with him. You have to consult him on a consistent basis, concerning every decision. "What would Jesus do" has to be more than a catchy phase on a wristband, but you must live your life with this question at the forefront of your mind. Before you initiate, react or respond to any situation, make a point of asking God for his counsel, and do not move until you're sure he has responded. If God is not saying anything different, don't do anything different. Continue to seek him until you find him.

Challenged to Change

I challenge you to lay down this book for a few minutes and really think about the way you treat God on a consistent basis. If you can truly say that you give him his proper respect 100% of the time then you are free to move right to the next chapter. But if you know that you are not always attentive to God. If you know that you could do better with how you respond to him and what you do for him I challenge you to take a few minutes and rededicate yourself to him. *Dedication is not impeded by conditions.*

This means that no matter what state your life is in, you are making a commitment to consistently honor God without wavering!

If you show God that you can lift him up on both your good and bad days. If you show God that he has nothing to worry about - if he blesses you, you will not change on him. If you tell God this and then began to show him your dedication, I believe that you will begin to see things changing around you as you make this very important change from within. Start the process now...take a few minutes and let God know that he can depend on you no matter what comes! Then join me in the next chapter!

Chapter 7

Stress - Pride, Purpose and People!

Stress vs. Pride

2 Cor 12:7-9 (KJV) - And lest I should be exalted above measure by the abundance of the revelations, a thorn in the flesh was given to me, a messenger of Satan to buffet me, lest I be exalted above measure.

To buffet means to worry someone constantly or to bring stress to a person's life. Paul is declaring that God put stress in his life. Why would God do this? Paul has survived through and accomplished a great deal at this point in his life, and because of this God knew that Paul would eventual become prideful and began to think too highly of himself. The bible points out the danger of this in Proverbs 16:18, where it says that "pride goes before destruction". If you recall, during the preface, I explained that there are people who have achieved a measure of success in life, and because of this they refuse to make changes. This stance is usually taken due to a curtain measure of pride one takes in their accomplishments. There is absolutely nothing wrong with being proud of yourself, but when that pride causes you to consider your own desires above the will of God for your life you have reached a destructive place.

Allow me to share this with you. A few years ago I had an automobile that no longer functioned properly. Because the cost of the repairs exceeded to value of the car I chalked it up as a loss and parked the car in my garage. A few months later I went to purchase a new car. The salesmen asked if I had another car to trade in. I told him yes. I had the car in my garage that had been sitting for months. I told him about the need for repairs but it didn't matter. He said that all he needed was a "trade in" to make the deal for my new car work. So I scheduled a time for them to pick up the car. My plan was to back it out of the driveway and park it in front of the house. But when I went to start the car the battery was dead. "No big deal" I thought, "I'll just give it a boast and start it up". When I went to boast it the charge would not take. The car had been sitting so long that the battery was no longer any good. "No big deal" I thought, "I will just go and purchase another battery, start the car and back it out". So I replaced the battery and the car started. But when I attempted to put the car in reverse the gear would not come out of park. I remember being told that one way to fix this was to turn the steering wheel from left to right, but after a few turns the steering wheel locked! The car was stuck in park with no mobility. In order to turn the car in the tow truck driver had to drag it out of the garage, which I'm sure caused even more damage. When I told the tow truck driver about the problems I had with the car he said something that stuck with me to this day, "a car can become damaged just by sitting in one place for too long! If it does not change positions from time to time, the mechanics of the vehicle will ware, rust and become dysfunctional". I am not one of those people who believe that cares have feelings, but it felt as if my car simply refused to be moved. It had become comfortable in its warm spot in my garage and when the time came to change it simply refused to be moved. The car had traveled over 100,000 thousand miles, so it had served its purpose in the past. But now it was meant to fulfill a greater purpose by trading in its present position to make room for something new!

The effects of pride can have the same effect on people. It can cause a person to sit in one place for so long that they become stubborn and complacent; so much until they refuse to move from a certain place, even when their time in that place has passed. **Isaiah 2:12 (NIV) says "The LORD Almighty has a day in store for all the proud and lofty, for all that is exalted (and they will be humbled)"**. I struggled for days attempting to move my car from my garage but it would not budge. No matter how hard I tried. It would not start. It would not switch. It would not turn. There eventually came **a day** when I had to drag it out and carry it away. My friend, if you allow pride to have the same effect on your willingness to change I fear you will face the same outcome. Change will happen in either 1 of 4 ways...

- ❖ Change will happen around you.
- ❖ Change will happen in spite of you.
- ❖ Change will happen at your expense.

Or

- ❖ Change will happen for you and within of you!

If you allow pride to set in I am sure that you will encounter at least one of the first there options. *God will not allow your pride to get in the way of progress. Either you can be a part of it or you will be a casualty of it*. When I dragged the car it almost immediately destroyed both of the front tires. Had it been dragged any further it would have surely caused more damage. When you feel pride setting in remember these words: *Change is going to happen...you can either be humble and move with it or be prideful and be dragged away by it. The choice is yours*.

God understands the drastic impacts that pride can have our ability to change. For this reason he placed a thorn inside of each one of us. This thorn is meant to cause constant worry, in an effort to remind us that we cannot take so much pride in ourselves that we become detached from God's purpose for our lives.

Stress Has a Purpose

As you walk this road to change it is important that you remember this: *change does not always mean that stressful things are going to be taken out of your life. Sometimes the only way to combat stressful situations is to change how you deal with them. You can't always change it, but you can always change you*! If you continue to allow stress to drive you to pity, frustration and depression you run the risk of being consumed by those feelings for the rest of your life. *But if you change the way you react to stress, change the way you respond to stress, and change the way you allow stress to impact you, you can have an even bigger victory!*

It's easy to move when an obstacle has been removed, but the true power of God in your life is shown when you can move ahead in spite of the obstacles standing in your way!

In 2 Corinthians 12, Paul declares that God's strength is made perfect in his (Paul's) weakness. *In order to change you have to recognize that your strength is insufficient; you can't do it all but you can do it in spite of*! *You must change the thinking that you need certain stresses removed before you can do greater things*. Paul declares that he asked God to remove his thorn (stress) 3 times and each time was told no. That gives us the inclination that waiting for stress to pass could be pointless. If God refuses to remove your stress it only means that your stress has a purpose. It is meant to ignite your passion. It is meant to influence you to switch gears from park to drive! It is meant to motivate you to turn your life in a different direction.

God told Paul that the grace he provided was sufficient, as we've previously discussed sufficient means just enough. *Even though we strive for more than just grace we must take advantage of the grace that we now possess. If you want change to take place in your life you must look beyond the discomfort of stress and believe that no matter what you're dealing with you have just enough to gain more than enough! Remember this: If God doesn't take your stress away that only means that you can make it with it!*

Challenged to Change

This next challenge is a bit different. This time I don't want you to speak to God, but I want you to take a few moments and speak over yourself. Tell yourself that you will not allow stress to stop you! Tell yourself that you are done waiting for the perfect time…the time is now! You will not wait for stress to pass, but you will fight through it by striving toward change even while stress is present! Tell yourself "you can do this…in spite of…"! Take a few minutes and encourage yourself and let's continue our conversation in the next chapter!

Chapter 8

The Temporary Avoidance of Others

Believe it or not there was another benefit of stress revealed to me. An emotional symptom called "the avoidance of others". I added the word "temporary" because interaction with people is a must, but it can and must be regulated when you are attempting to change. I believe that God has to send stress at times because stress is only thing that will cause us to truly examine and adjust the ways that we interact with people.

- ❖ Stress will pull us away from social media.
- ❖ Stress will cause you to reevaluate your relationships.
- ❖ Stress will cause you to examine your hangouts and extracurricular activities.
- ❖ Stress will force you to put your cell phone down.
- ❖ Stress will help you to see that people are walking all over you and it's time for you to stand up for yourself.

In a nut shell, stress is sometimes the only thing that God can use to make you see that you're talking to, becoming friends with, following, liking, supporting or even sleeping with the enemy!

Have you ever had to cut someone out of your life; and the reason had nothing to do with you not liking them, loving them or wanting them in your life? You wanted all of those things but you had to cut them loose anyway because the stress they added to your life was far too much for you to bear! Well allow me to reveal something to you...are you ready? Here it goes. The person that stresses you out has probably never been any good for you. It's a good chance they've been holding you back, throwing you off track or even killing you slowly ever since the first day they met you. _People will throw your life off track and never even realize they are doing anything wrong to you; they are just being themselves_. And because of this you must be very mindful of all of your interactions.

Let's take Facebook for instance. I love Facebook. Of all the social media outlets it has by far been the biggest contributor to the success of my church! But I noticed about a year or so ago that I was becoming a Facebook junkie! I'd spend hour's just flipping through and reading posts. Whenever I went to post a comment I would get anxiety because I wanted it to be perfect and grab the attention of the reader. It would take me hours sometimes to get my comment right. When I finally posted, I'd go back and check constantly for likes, and I'd be hurt or frustrated when I didn't get them. I had it bad; until one day I realized I had wasted so much time, watching, communicating, and seeking "likes" from people. I love all of my Facebook friends, but if they never like another comment that I post "life still goes on". If my Facebook firends do like my posts that's great, but now what? It's not about the amount of people that like you, it's about the amount that support you. If I post a flyer, it's great if they like it, but I know they support me when they repost it or support the event in person.

The point I'm making is that we will bend over backward to get people to like us. There are people, everyday, humiliating themselves on social media just to get someone to like them. Why? The thought process is "if you like me, that means you approve of me. You approve of what I say, you approve of how I look, you approve of what I'm doing with my time and your approval makes me feel validated". That's good but it's also dangerous, because what happens when they don't like what you post? Docs that make you are any less valid? It will if you place your value in the thoughts of people. You have to know that you are validated rather they like it or not. You have to know that you are great at what you do rather someone approves of it or not. And if you're not great you have to know that too, and don't allow people to stunt your growth by giving you "pity likes "on social media or in life!

Know the Issues of the People around You

Usually stress is caused by an ongoing continuous incident that begins to weigh on you at an unbearable level. It takes time for us to see that characteristics in others that we once considered to be cute, fun, harmless, or even sexy have been the source of our undoing all along. In many cases, even though we know that a person or thing is no good for us we find a way to live with the headaches that they bring. As you progress toward change you must accept the fact that you are going to need people around you. You must also understand that those people are going to have issues.

Jesus had 12 disciples. One of them continually resisted his warnings (Peter), 2 of them wanted to sit on either side him - sharing his authority (John and James), one of them was a doubter (Thomas), another betrayed him and turned him over to his enemies (Judas), and all of them scattered and left him when the Pharisees took him away to be unjustly tried! Not to mention the angry mob that called for the freedom of the guilty Barabbas over the innocent Savior. Those people were afraid of Barabbas, but they were so filled with un-warranted spite and contempt for Jesus that they chose someone who could have killed them over someone who wanted to save them. Jesus walked with individuals who had issues, and at times made his life more difficult than it had to be. But we must remember that Jesus picked these individuals himself, knowing their issues. And that's the key! *You have to know who you're walking with! You have to know their issues and their weakness, and you have to be sure that if they must stay close to you, you never let them close enough to impede your progress*.

Know When to Create Space

When Jesus went to the Garden of Gethsemane to pray before the night of his trial, he left his disciples in one place and went further to pray alone. Jesus was stressed, because he knew he had a long brutal road ahead of him, and he tells his disciples "you stay here and watch, while I go and pray alone". I believe that Jesus is trying to teach us in that scripture that stress and people are not always a good combination! *The "temporary" avoidance of others is a symptom and a benefit of stress, because it causes you to evaluate the importance of certain people at certain times* _and to leave the crowed behind when necessary_. Every person is not meant to be with you at every instance. This applies even to your supporters. There are times when you are going to have to break away and handle your responsibilities on your own.

At this moment I am in my basement, locked in my den, writing this book. It's a Friday night. My wife and two sons are upstairs. This would be a perfect opportunity for a family night or a date night, but I'm here writing to you. Hear what I'm telling you. I love my family more than I love myself, and that's why I'm here writing and not out with them at this moment. That is why the door is closed behind me and I'm off limits to them at this time. If I love them I have to do the best that I can do for them. I have to work toward our future, even if it means a little sacrifice. We've had plenty of family nights and date nights, and we will have many many more! I am not saying that family time and dating time are not important. **You MUST have those times set aside or your family will change for the worst.** My point is _if you're not careful, you can even allow the people you love to draw you away from the changes that you need to make in your life._

You can be so consumed with spending time with your family until you put no extra time and effort into making life better for your family. Parents all over the world use their children as excuses for why they never pursue their dreams. *If you want to change your present situation, you are going to have to evaluate the time you give to all people...including your loved ones*. And let me tell you something, *the most stressful avoidance of people comes when you have to avoid those that you love in order to pursue your change*. Extra hours at work, long hours at school, nights and weekends dedicated to getting a business off the ground; those sacrifices are tough when you have people that you love and hate to be away from. But if you want change, there are times when you're going to have to still away...just for a time.

At the end of Jesus' earthly assignment he tells the disciples, **"in my Father's house there are many mansions. I go to prepare a place for you" (John 14:2, KJV)!** In other words there are great things out there to obtain, but in order for you to have them I have to leave you so that I may prepare them for you! He continues to say **"if I go and**

prepare a place for you, I will come again and receive you unto myself; that where I am, there ye may be also".

What Jesus saying here is that even though I must separate with you to prepare something greater I'm coming back for you! Notice he doesn't allow the disciples to come and prepare it with him! Why - because *if I want change there are certain things I have to do independent of the people around me*! The disciples had not completed their own work...they really hadn't even started their own work. So how could they be of assistance to Jesus in Heaven? They could not, so he had to leave them behind, just for a time.

My friends, this part of change is tough...arguably the toughest part of change. *When we become attached to people, even those that we know are no good; it is sometimes the toughest decision in the world to separate*. But you have to trust that God will put the right people in your life at the right time. You must trust that he will not only reward you for your changes but he will also reward the people around you! Even though the disciples weren't always the most faithful after Jesus rose from the grave he went and showed himself to them. He would not ascend to

Heaven until he had seen his friends one last time. Before he rose from the grave - the last time they had seen him he was beaten and bloodied. But after he rose they got a chance to see him healed, powerful, and confident; as a matter of fact the bible says that when Jesus came out of the grave the disciples didn't recognize him right away. I believe that was because he looked so good! He didn't look like the beaten and shattered man they had seen just a few days prior...he was change for the better!

Challenge to Change

I challenge you now to again put down this book, and have a conversation with God. Ask him about the people in your life...

- ❖ Who's good for me?
- ❖ Who needs to go?
- ❖ How much time should I devote to certain people?
- ❖ How do I balance the changes I need to make with the family that I must attend to?

Really pray about this my friend. Seek God about it now. Ask him for the strength to make changes in this area. Ask him to reveal who's really on your side. You need to know because your ability change is going to weigh heavily on whom you have in your life and how you interact with them. Talk to God about that now, and then come back and talk to me in the next chapter.

Chapter 9

Stress Tests

James 1:3 - Knowing that the <u>testing</u> of your faith produces patience (NKJV).

Before any new car hits the showroom floor, car makers test their vehicles using all types of methods. The most well know test is the "crash test". This is when an auto maker purposely designs and creates a car just to crash it into a wall. The point of the crash is not to gage what the impact does to the car, but the test is designed to gage the impact the crash will have on the driver! The automobile is not released until the auto maker is satisfied of the following…

- ❖ The driver is able to survive the crash.
- ❖ After the crash is over the driver is still sitting securely where they have been placed.
- ❖ The driver is still physically, emotionally and mentally stable after the crash.

God uses stress in the same manor. 1 Corinthians 10:13 says "God will never let you down; he'll never let you be pushed past your limit" (MSG). Though God will never push you past your limits he will sometimes push you to your limits. His reason for this is to test your faith to ensure it can survive the most dangerous of situations.

Healed through Stress

2 Chronicles 7:13-14 (NIV) - "When I shut up the heavens so that there is no rain, or command locusts to devour the land or send a plague among my people, if my people, who are called by my name, will humble themselves and pray and seek my face and turn from their wicked ways, then I will hear from heaven, and I will forgive their sin and will heal their land.

In this scripture God makes a point to inform us that he will bring stressful situations upon us. But the stress is meant to gain certain reactions. While you are attempting to change you must remember that your stress is merely a test. And you pass the test by recognizing the following…

- ❖ Stress is meant to bring about humility.
- ❖ Stress is meant to encourage prayer.
- ❖ Stress is meant to provoke the seeking of God.
- ❖ Stress is meant to motivate the discontinuation of undesirable behavior (wickedness).

When you respond appropriately to stress God promises that he will do 2 things on your behalf. *He will hear and he will heal!* Notice God does not say that he will fix the land but he specifically and intentionally uses the word "heal". When something is fix it can be operational immediately after, but the healing process takes time, even after the issue has been fixed.

Several years ago I tore my Achilles tendon which required surgery. The surgery only took an hour... two hours at the most, and after it was done my tendon was fixed. Even though it was fixed I still could not walk, stand or move it; and the pain I experienced after the surgery was even greater than when it was initially torn! Much greater! No mobility in my tendon, but it was still fixed. How could this be? Even though the issue was fixed it still needed to heal? The inability to walk, move, and stand, along with the extreme pain was all a part of the healing process; without the healing there would be no movement, no mobility, and most importantly no release from the pain.

My friend, you must understand that change will be almost impossible if you do not allow the healing process to take place. There are going to be times where you feel that you have no mobility in life. You will change your approach to your finances and you will still not be able to do the things you've dreamed of doing. You will change your approach to your marriage and your spouse will not immediately respond as you envisioned. You will change the way you deal with people and they will still hurt you. You will change your relationship with God and you will still feel as if you're being punished. When this happens you must remember that these things are not evidence that things have not change, but these are the things that take place during the course of change. You must remember that change takes time. *The decision to change can happen in an "instant", but the process of change takes being "persistent"*. And one of the main areas where persistence must be shown is in the area of faith.

Through surgery my tendon had been fixed. The doctor that did the surgery told me it was fixed. But it did not feel like it had been fixed; in fact it felt worse than when I came into the hospital. It didn't appear to be fixed; it had swollen up terribly and had stitches everywhere. It didn't function as if it was fixed, I couldn't stand, walk or move it. But in spite of all of those things I still had to have faith in what I had been told and believe that I would see the results of the surgery as the healing took place. Your process of change is going to be very similar to the process of surgery. Things are not allows going to feel, look or operate as if they have changed, especially in the beginning stages. But you must have faith in what the doctor has told you, the doctor being God of course.

Today I have full strength and mobility. I can stand, walk, run and jump, I can even slam dunk a basket again. That tells me that the surgery was not botched; it worked just as the doctor said it would. It didn't happen over night but it did happen over time. The doctor did the surgery but I had to believe in his work and commit to his process. Just as I had to stay faithful to what the doctor had said and done, I also had to stay faithful to my commitment. No matter how it looked, felt or functioned, I had to continue to believe that it was fixed, and that the results would began to manifest over time. You are going to have to hold to the same faith in God and in yourself. You must believe that the changes you make will **soon** manifest into what you have been promised.

In this section of the book I sought to explain that stress can be a good thing because it keeps you pursuing God's plan for your life. But allow me also to inform you that God's plans do not conclude without his purpose being fulfilled. If his purpose for stress is to get you to do something that you still have not done it could very well mean that you will continue to be stressed until you give God what he seeks from you. I say "why wait"?

Challenged to Change

I challenge you; if you're tired of dealing with stressful situations, put down this book and acknowledge God in the ways describe in 2 Chronicles. Humble yourself in his presence, pray, seek his face, and ask him to give you the strength to turn for any undesirable ways. If you do this he promises to hear and heal! Take as long as you need...get heard, get healed, and then get back to the next chapter! We've got a lot more to talk about!

Chapter 10

Too Much Stress

According to WebMD some stress is beneficial, but too much stress is not. "Too much stress can wear you down and make you sick, both mentally and physically". I agree that some stress is good, but when I went through the symptoms, as I said, I only found 2 out of 26 that could be used beneficially. It is clear that the negative effects of stress outweigh the benefits. You may be thinking that this section of the book is not for you because you don't feel stressed. But according to this same article "recognizing stress symptoms may be harder than you think, because most of us are so used to being stressed, we often don't know we are stressed until we are at the breaking point". Not feeling stressed could be evidence that stress has overtaken you, and you just haven't recognized it.

Stress comes in 4 core symptoms; *emotional, physical, cognitive* and *behavioral*. And for someone reading this book one or more of these symptoms, are areas of needed change in your life. In order to recognize your true need for change you must first recognize the true source of your stress.

Emotional Changes

Someone needs to change your emotional state because you cannot continue spending the majority of your time fighting. You are fighting at home, you fight at work, you fight with people, you even battle with your own thoughts, feelings and emotions; your life is one fight after another and it must change. You have to change your emotional state because you cannot continue having mood swings, causing your atmosphere to be uncomfortable and your personality to be deemed unstable.

You have to change your emotional state because you cannot continue to struggle with "depression". Depression will turn your shortcomings into your masters instead of your motivators. Your short comings should motivate you to make plans and adjustments, and push you to be better next time. But when depression sets in it causes every struggle, every misstep, and every mistake to hold you in an emotional state of captivity. It paralyzes your feelings to the point that even though you have the activities of your limbs you have no emotional desire to move.

You must change you emotional state because you've cried long enough. You've been sad long enough. You've been reliving previous life occurrences that have manipulated your emotions long enough. Death of a loved one, divorce, family issues, physical abuse, financial setbacks; these are just a few examples of events that may have left you in an emotionally handicapped state. You cry uncontrollably, you're angry for no present reason, your bitter with people who have nothing to do with your present disposition, you refuse to trust and depend on anyone but yourself. If you've felt or are feeling any of these symptoms your emotional condition must change...immediately!

Physical Changes

Stress will cause you to "let yourself go". Bad eating habits, allowing illnesses to linger; stress even has the ability to create illnesses in your body. Terrible headaches, stomach ulcers, high blood pressure, and the inability to rest even when you are asleep among other things. *Your physical condition is essential to where God is trying to take you*! You cannot continue to allow stress to alter your physically condition or appearance, because those things may in turn alter the places that you are destined to go. God needs you healthy and looking well so that you can carry out and represent the great blessing that he has in store for your life. If you look in the mirror and you don't like what you see you must commit to changing it. You have to look the part, even if you haven't gotten the part yet. You have to dress for the job you want, not for the job you have. You have to present yourself as someone who is blessed beyond measure, not someone who needs a blessing, even if you do in fact need a blessing.

Recently I experienced a back injury. While working out at the gym I placed too many weights on a certain machine. When I went to lift the weights I could feel the strain in my back, but my "ego" would not allow me to give in. So I lifted the weights anyway, against my better judgment, and I end up badly straining my back. It was terrible. I could barely walk; I couldn't stand up straight or sit for long periods of time. The pain was so terrible that it caused my hands to shake from time to time. I took many different pain killers and muscle relaxers, but none of them worked. While I was suffering and couldn't understand why the medication wouldn't take, my mother told me something that I had not given much attention to. She said that the pain in my back was not only due to my injury but it was also due to stress. I was so focused on the injury that I never gave any thought that it was stress that caused my physical condition to be negatively impacted. So I made the decision that I would not take any more medication. But instead I would stretch, exercise and continue to move through the pain and the stress. I would force myself to stand up straight, no matter how badly it hurt. I would take long walks at lunch time, even with a bad limp. I would still drive, I would still run, I would not call off of work, and I would still preach at my church on Sunday. I would not allow that stress to continue to impact me physically. I could not control the pain, but I could control rather or not I would allow it to hinder my day to day life. Before long my back was back to normal without me even recognizing it. I had begun to ignore the pain so much that I didn't even notice when it had left me. And it all happened after I stopped allowing the stress and pain to dictate my movements. *<u>I had to change my mentality from "I can't do it because it hurts" to "I will do it even if it hurts"</u>*!

When I changed my approach and my mentality toward stress, the condition of my body fell in line and change accordingly. And I believe that this same change is just as simple for you. When you change how you allow pain and stress to dictate your movements your body will began to resurrect itself. The stress in my back had me walking, standing and moving strangely, but when I made up my mind that stress would not have its way over my body any more, my body responded and became whole again. If you make the same decision I believe you will have the same result!

Cognitive Changes

The word "cognitive" describes the state of your mentality. Someone needs cognitive changes because your mind is racing, you cannot focus, you are constantly using poor judgment, you are always pessimistic…you just don't like anything. You're thinking needs to improve. You're decision making needs to improve. You must become stable and stop going back and forth with your positions in life.

 A few chapters ago I mention Romans chapter 12, verse 2; let's take a look at that scripture one more time. It advises us to "be not *conformed* to this world, but to be *transformed* by the renewing of your mind"! That word "transformed" makes me think of a carton I loved as a child and a series of movies that I have enjoyed as an adult called "Transformers"! The "Transformers" are alien robots that can change to take on the shape of earthly vehicles.

With that in mind, consider this: If you were to go outside right now and take a look at your vehicle, it looks very long because it sits horizontally, but if you were to somehow stand it up vertically the vehicle would not stand any more than 8 to 12 feet high. Not much higher than a basketball hoop at best. But in the movies, when these transformers turn themselves into their true form they become taller than buildings and sky scrapers. Do you know why that is? When they become vehicles they are really *conforming* to the world that they live in. They are blending into their environment, attempting to hide who they really are. But when they transform they become even bigger and taller than they should conceivably be by human standards. This difference between *conforming* and *transforming* has the same effect on your life. <u>When you conform your thinking to that of this world you limit yourself to doing nothing more than blending in - being unnoticed, nothing special. But when you transform your thinking to that which is Godly, and change your mind to consistently think of things above, it makes you larger and taller than what you should conceivably be</u>. Godly thinking reveals who you are in your true and most powerful form; someone who has the power and authority to tread upon serpents, to speak and watch what you speak come to pass, to lay hands on the sick and watch them recover! Conformation keeps you grounded, but transformation makes you greater! Which state of thinking will you chose?

Behavioral Changes

Behavior is defined by how a person acts, but the interesting thing about the definition is that it sights behavior as an action or response to stimulation. To be stimulated means to be aroused or excited. Someone needs a behavioral change, not just to regulate your actions but to regulate your responses when you are aroused or excited. There are some who simply cannot control themselves when they find themselves in highly stimulating situations. For some it may be a simple disagreement that evolves into an all out battle, simply because you cannot accept someone else's differences in thoughts or opinions. You always have to be right, and if another person does not agree, you will not let up until they do. Some will even go as far as being verbally abrasive or physically violent in order to get their point across. For someone else, behavior is defined by the lackadaisical ways in which you respond. When something isn't going as you would like you do nothing to change it. Instead you wallow and sulk, or even worse, you act as if you are not bothered at all and you continue to behave as if nothing has happened. Others may do poorly controlling the arousal they feel when they are around someone they are physically attracted to. The issue with this is that we are not always physically attracted to the right kind of people.

My friend, if you want to see change take place in your life you must either learn or ask God for the strength to give you the ability to control yourself at all times! You cannot be a "hot head", and you cannot have a "hot body". You cannot be easily moved, aroused or excited; not by the foolishness, stubbornness, or even the niceness or attractiveness of another individual. Jesus said in **Luke chapter 21 (KJV), "in your patience possess your soul"**. He said this as part of a warning to the disciples that they would be accused by strangers, betrayed by friends and family, even beaten and killed because of their commitment to him. Still in all of these things Jesus admonishes them to keep it together, stay cool, stay calm, be patience; because in spite of everything that would happen to them "not a hair on their heads would parish". In other words, as long as they stayed calm, even in the toughest of situations, they would be the survivors when everything was said and done.

If I haven't conveyed it clearly enough to this point allow me to say it as plainly as I can, "**your change is not going to be easy".** It is going to put you in the tightest of spots and bring about the most aggravating of circumstances. Odds are, you have been the way that you are now for a number of years, and your flesh, your environment, your family, and your enemies (spiritual and natural) are not going to let you go without an incredible fight. Through it all you have to control yourself. You have to bring your flesh under subjection. You cannot be a "loose cannon", ready to explode at the light of a match. You have to know what pushes your buttons and stay away from those things. You have to know who drives you crazy and stay away from those people. And please don't get this misconstrued, *what you are doing is not running, it is not hiding, and it is not* *weakness;* as a matter of fact it shows more strength to show restraint than it does to give release.

James 4:7 instructs to "submit to God and resist the devil". *The devil is not a red man with horns and a pointed tail. The devil is the main spiritual agent of temptation. He is the voice, the urge and feeling which provokes you into partaking in negative behaviors that have the potential to follow you for the rest of your life*. Behaviors have a way of lingering and leaving lasting repercussions. And fair or not, the systems of life are set up to judge you based on how you've *behaved* in the past, instead of how you're *behaving* in the present. Why do you think creditors pull credit reports, or employers pull background and criminal history checks? Because they want to gage how you will behave in the future by how you have behaved in the past. It doesn't matter how much you try to convince them that you are a different person now, they only go by what your reports tell them. It's time to change your report!

It will take time, but it must start somewhere. Every day that you behave better is one more day of separation from the person that you used to be. In the beginning it will be a struggle, because you are changing into a new person, but the more you behave better the more "better" just becomes who you are. The rule for credit reports is that it takes 7 years for a negative item to drop off. But I have found that if you just show better financial behaviors for a year or so creditors will start to work with you. 2 or 3 years of good behavior, along with steady income, will get you approved for just about anything. The point I am making is that even though the threshold is supposed to be 7 years, if you began to change your behaviors the time that you will be penalized for your past will be less than anticipated.

Struggle with Your Symptom

Now that we have examine the symptoms and reasoning behind stress it is time to speak against them. If you are experiencing any of these four symptoms the need for change in your life is vital. You cannot and will not see better days if you have emotional, cognitive, physical or behavioral issues that have not been addressed. Your weakness will always be your undoing. Sure, we will all always struggle with something, but the key to dealing with an issue is in your willingness to struggle with it. The word struggle means to make forceful or violent efforts to get free of restraint or constriction. When you consider the definition you must admit that struggling with something is really a good thing. It means that you are attempting to fight something off of you! *<u>You cannot experience change if you are not always struggling (fighting off) your issue</u>*.

Challenged to Change

I challenge you now to search yourself. Discover your symptom of stress, and commit to fighting it off of you with everything you've got! Start the fight right now with prayer. Not just any pray but pray in a manner that lets your issue know that it is in for a fight. No more giving in, no more lying down, you want change and you are ready to fight for it! Remember at the beginning of the chapter I said that you could be stressed and not even realize it. Not only could you be stressed and not realize it, but the effects of stress could be having more of a negative impact on you than you realize. Don't risk it. I challenge you now to put down this book and declare war on you symptom! Pray against the power and the impact of your symptom of stress in your life! Pray against it like you've never prayed before and then come back and talk to me in the next chapter.

Chapter 11

Why Am I Stressed?

This is not a book about stress; this book is about importance of change. So why have we focused so much on stress in this section…because stress is something that you cannot avoid! It is going to hit you even if you don't recognize it or understand fully what's happening to you. According to WebMD "recognizing stress symptoms may be harder than you think, because most of us are so used to being stressed, we often don't know we are stressed until we are at *the breaking point*". Rather you call it stress or you recognize it as your breaking point, you are going to be pushed by the symptoms of stress to make changes in your life! The point is not to attempt to avoid stress, because you can't, but to find out how to use it to work in your favor.

Stress vs. Faith

Mark 4:35-41 (KJV) tells us about a day when Jesus and his disciples set out on the Sea of Galilee. While they are sailing a storm breaks out. Mind you, *a storm breaks out as soon as they left with Jesus.* Remember this: <u>storms are not evidence that God is not with you…quite the contrary…the appearance of a storm is sometimes confirmation that God is on your side</u>. The disciples leave with Jesus, a storm breaks out, and they become afraid; but Jesus is asleep and does not wake up. So they run and wake Jesus, and under immense fear and stress they ask him "do you not care that we are about to perish".

Had I been a disciple on the boat I quite possibly would have asked the same question. I am a living disciple today, and I can honestly say that I have asked that question many times during my past trails. But as I studied the scripture Jesus brought something to my attention. When it came to the question of his caring, he asked me to read verse 37 again and then consider my question again. Verse 37 says "there rose a great storm of wind and waves beat into the ship, so that it was full". The ship was full of water. When have you ever heard of ship being full of water, in the middle of the sea and not sinking? This ship was full of water, in the middle the sea and it never sunk to the bottom!

Just as the ship was full of water, there have been times when our lives have been full of problems that have caused us to experience the fullness of stress, or as you may call it "the breaking point". The breaking point is defined as the moment of greatest strain at which someone or something gives way. Being full of water this ship should have reached its breaking point, but because Jesus was onboard the fullness could not cause the ship to break and the people did not drown. If you look back over your life I am sure you can admit that you should have drowned a long time ago. Sure there have been times where you were drowning, but God has never allowed the storm to overtake you! He reached in and pulled you out. He kept you afloat until you made it to dry land. This is how you know he cares.

Just as the disciples asked Jesus if he cared, we've asked or wondered the same. We have a tendency, when things don't seem to go our way, to take on a "why me" or a "poor me" mentality; but notice something in our scripture. When Jesus reprimands the disciples he asked them "why are you so fearful, how is it that you have no faith"? I believe that the power of that storm was directly connected to the stress, fearfulness and lack of faith shown by the disciples. The more they allowed their faith to wither and their stress and fear to grow the stronger the storm became. That is quite possibly another reason why Jesus did not move right away, because he knew that all they had to do was to show faith and fight off fear and the storm would have passed on its own. And just as I believe that for the disciples I believe that for you as well. *The storms in your life are directly connected to the faith that you exercise. When your faith is weak your storm is strong, but as your faith is strengthened your storms will weaken*.

Jesus gives us the key for how to deal with the storm. The bible says that he rose up, rebuked the winds, and said unto the sea "Peace be still". Notice the word peace in the scripture begins with a capital P, but it is not at the beginning of the sentence. Words are only capitalized when they are at the beginning of a sentence or when they represent a person, place or thing. Jesus calling on Peace to be still meant that peace was in the atmosphere, it was just not yet brought under subjection to his will. Jesus didn't speak to the storm he spoke to the Peace within the storm. A key ingredient to change is having the ability to show increased faith and to minimize fear in the midst of a storm. How do I do this...*stop speaking to the storm and speak to the peace within it*! You must not allow your peace to run wild. Jesus speaks to peace as if it is a noun, not a feeling or a notion, but a person, place or thing, and he commands it rise up and to do its job!

Challenged to Change

I challenge you to put down this book, take a moment and do the same. We have a habit of speaking to our storms. We talk about what we're going through or what we're dealing with on a regular basis. But this time I challenge you not to speak to the storm but to speak to the peace within it. Storms are supposed to rage...that's what they do...but peace also has a job, and you must speak to it, and bring it under subjection to your authority through Christ Jesus. Take a few moments and speak to your Peace! Command it to be still in your family, command it to be still in your heart, command it to be still in your finances! Take a few moments and speak to your peace and then come back and speak to me in the next section of our reading!

CHANGE or DIE

PART 3

THE BELIEF IN CHANGE

Chapter 12

How Do I Change

As we continue to discuss change it is important that we understand how change is brought about. How do we change? We all want to change but the million dollar question is "how do we make it happen"? The bible gives us the key, in Romans chapter 12, where it simply informs us that we are transformed (changed), by the renewing of our minds! New mind, new you! New mind, new behaviors! New mind, new results! But what happens when your mind is in order, but you still do the opposite of what we know to be right? What happens when you know what's right, you agree with what's right, and you believe in what's right but every time you're approached with a certain situation you continue to make the wrong choice? You know that certain people are not good for you, but you continue to maintain a relationship with them. You know that certain behaviors lead to certain repercussions but you continue to indulge. So many strong urge's, so many extenuating circumstances; how do we overcome these things to obtain the change that we seek? In an effort to answer this question allow me to provide you with 4 influences that will help you to finally grasp and commit to the concept of change.

Once you've Changed, Continue To Change…Once Is Not Enough

The mistake that most people make when it comes to change is the belief that once they've changed they never need to change again. This is the furthest thing from the truth. Change must be revisited, revised, and refreshed on a consistent basis. My Bishop J. Drew Sheard would often say that "salvation (spiritual change) is a process; it means that today I am better than I was yesterday, and tomorrow

I will be better than I am today". *The change that you seek will not happen overnight, but it will and **must** happen over time. While in the process of change you must think "progression", not "satisfaction"*.

The best way to keep this in mind is to consider the progression of Satan. When we are first introduced to Satan in the book of Genesis, he is just a small serpent, but by the time we see him again at the end in the book of Revelation he is a large dragon! Always keep this in mind: *You must constantly revisit change because you face an enemy that is constantly changing*!

You cannot fight a new battle with old weapons. You cannot fight a new world order with an old school mentality. As long as you face an ever-changing world, and an ever- changing enemy you must not view change as something that you do once and never again. Day by day, year by year, experience by experience, you must continue to keep positive change at the forefront of your thinking. Always remember, your enemy is ever changing and progressing rather you chose to do the same or not.

You Must Become Tired of You!

You are never really going to change until you really become tired of being "who" and "where" you are. In Acts chapter 9, when Jesus calls Paul he does not initially change him, but instead he challenges him. He asks "Paul, why do you persecute me? Why do you kick against the pricks"? To "kick against the pricks" means to hurt oneself by persisting in useless resistance and behaviors. My friend, if you are going to see change come to pass in your life, you are going to have to answer the same type of tough questioning.

- ❖ Why do you continue to do things that hurt you?
- ❖ Why do you continue to maintain certain relationships when those relationships have been proven to be toxic for you?
- ❖ Why do you continue to settle for a job when you've got a multi-million dollar idea on the inside of you?

We all tell ourselves that we need to change, but do we ever ask ourselves why we won't change even when what we are doing does more harm than good to our lives. Honestly, have you asked yourself "Why can't I change when I know that my life is not what it's supposed to be"? The answer is simply: *you will change when you've finally had enough*.

I mentioned in the preface that the problems of life are not always motivations for change. Those aspects of life that are killing us, or driving us insane, even when we hold the key and the authority to end one thing and start something greater; *until we are truly fed up with the present state of our lives we will never truly commit to change*. When we try to change - if our hearts are not totally committed and our tolerance for our present state has not reached its limits - we will eventually revert back to being "who" and "what" we are today.

When Jesus encountered Paul, who was at that time named Saul, he did not immediately send him into the world as a disciple. Instead, he took his sight and sent him to a house on a street called "Straight". Paul sat in a room alone for 3 days with no sight, no food, and no one to talk to. What was the point of this? I believe it was done so that

Paul could take the time to reexamine his life. To really think about the person he had been, the things that he had done, and the commitment to change he had just made.

Problems are different for everyone, but the reactions to problems are universal...

- Drinking
- Smoking,
- Drugs,
- Infidelity,
- Fornication,
- Addiction,
- Lack of patience
- Lack of planning
- Bad relationships
- Bad habits
- Irresponsibility
- Lying
- Stealing
- Lack of a solid relationship with God

I can almost guarantee that anything you need to change is intermingled with at least one of the things that I have just mentioned. These things may feel good to you or be familiar to you; but in time these behaviors chip away at your life until there's nothing left. *If you truly want change, you must take some time, as Paul did, and reflect on the negative ways that these things are impacting your life. If this time of reflection does not lead you to decide that you are fed up then unfortunately you are probably not prepared to change*. If you are not fed up, but you still want to change, don't lose hope, God can help you to see what you can't, if you allow him.

While Paul is sitting in the house, the Lord sends a disciple named Ananias to speak with him. God tells Ananias **"he will show Paul the great things he must suffer" (Acts 9:16, KJV)**. Notice, God says that he will **show** Paul what he must suffer while Paul is presently blind. Once Ananias ministers to Paul and touches him the scales fall from his eyes and he regains his sight. Sometimes we want to change, but we are just too wrapped up in that thing in our lives that needs to change. It becomes a way of life for us, a method of relaxation; some even earn their living doing things that must be changed. But just as God sent Ananias to Paul I believe that God has sent me to minster and to touch you in the same fashion. To help you to receive your sight so that you might see how you are harming yourself by staying as you are.

Change is about more than just new homes, new cars and new money. Change is about more than a renewed mind and a renewed body. <u>But the most important part of change is the discontinuing of processes that are destroying your life</u>. **God's desire for you is that you might live in peace and abundance (Malachi 3:10, KJV). His plans for you are of good and not of evil, to bring you to an expected end (Jeremiah 29:11, KJV). With God, even our struggles are beneficial in that his plan is for all things to work together for our good (Romans 8:28, KJV).** God wants great things for you, but it won't matter if you do not decide that you want those same things for yourself. When you become fed up with living with your same problems and issues, that's when you know that you want what God wants for you! Are you fed up yet?

Your Change Impacts Those around You

When Jesus calls Paul in Acts chapter 9, the bible says that there were others there with Paul, and they heard the voice of Jesus. They could not see him but they could hear his voice. Do you know why others heard the voice of Jesus when the words were only intended for Paul? Because the change that would take place within Paul would be a change that would not only affect him, but also those around him. *As you pursue change you must believe that your change is going to bring about a change in those who are connected to you….in a positive way!* Your house will be blessed, your children will be blessed, your close friends and most faithful supporters will all be blessed by your change! Sure there will be people that change for the worse, which we will discuss in just a few chapters, but you must believe that there will be more people who will be blessed by your gift. This has to be your motivation.

As you pursue change you are going to have days that will make you want to quit trying and retreat back to the safety and comfort of the past. You will be tempted to forget how miserable you were *"back then"*. You will be tempted to forget how unfulfilled you were *"back then"*. You will truly have days where you will rationalize returning to a past that you once desperately desired to escape, just to relieve yourself of the new pressures you will have to face. These are the days that you must consider how much of an impact your unwillingness to change will affect those whom you love and have been linked to by God; both naturally and spiritually. If you cannot change for yourself change for your children! If you cannot change for yourself change for your spouse! If you cannot change for yourself be motivated to change for all of those whom you hold dear! Remember this: God made it so that you deciding to stay as you are could mean that those closest to you may have to suffer! You may think that this is not fair, but it is actually an act of favor. God, in his genius, knew that if all we had to worry about were ourselves most of us would quit when change became difficult. But when you consider the way that your loved ones will be affected by your actions, or may have to suffer in the open for the things that you do in private, it should help you on the days that you want to scrap your plan to change and stay as you are.

Jesus saved Paul on the road to Damascus and then sent him to a street called "Straight". The Lord then sent Ananias to tell him that he had a greater calling on his life; to go into the world and preach the gospel. When Ananias came to encourage Paul to pursue a greater change, Paul could have simply told him that he was alright, right there on Straight Street. He could have kept his mouth shut, settled for his new salvation, and lived out his life taking care of only himself; but if he would have done this he would have left his destiny unfulfilled. Think of all of the great and profound books of the bible that have come from Paul. He has written, assisted, inspired or appeared in 15 of the 27 books of the New Testament. His change has produced some of the most quoted and influential scriptures of the bible. His ministry has been essential in making Christianity a worldwide phenomenon, spread throughout the nations. Countless numbers of people have been blessed, touched, changed, informed and inspired to live Godly due to Paul's ministry and guidance. Had Paul quit after Jesus saved him he could have been fine, but what state would the world be in today?

As I am writing this portion of the book my wife is proof reading Parts 1 and 2. Just moments ago, she sent me a text message that read as follows…

"Okay. I had time to read another portion of the book. I feel like it's going to help so many people".

How many people would this book have the potential to help if I still had these words floating around in my head? In order to change you have to take on the same thinking. You must consider not only yourself, but the great and wonderful things that your change will do for everyone you encounter. I use the word "encounter" because along with those closest to you, your gift will cause you to influence people whom you will never meet. I am a witness. My ministry through preaching has allowed me to have a positive influence on a multitude of people I may never meet; and my ministry through this book will allow me to positively impact millions more! If God can do this for me, he can do the same for you!

Change Yourself, Don't Cheat Yourself!

In order to see change, you must embrace this mentality: "If I don't change I am going to cheat myself out of my blessing"! You must tell this to yourself daily. I know that statement isn't very deep or profound, but you need to have it fixed in your mind and continuously spoken from your mouth. *If you truly desire change you must be able to tell yourself that YOU are going to cheat YOURSELF out of so many great things if YOU do not pursue change*. You have to have the ability, the strength and the humility to hold yourself accountable. Do you know how many people blame others for their struggles? Millions! Millions of people every day, upon examining their shortcomings, place the blame on everything from family and friends to society and government; some even blame God. Meanwhile, there are millions of other people who had to face the same obstacles, and have overcome them and are now living their dreams. The difference is that some people treat their obstacles as barriers and others treat them as opportunities. *My friend, if you want to seek change in your life you must change the way that you see the things that may be standing in your way. You have to resolve within yourself that those things are no longer obstacles but they are now opportunities.* A battle is no longer a reason for defeat but it is now an opportunity for victory! A family struggle is no longer a reason to walk away, but it is now an opportunity to prove your worth and your value to the people whom you hold most dear. A struggle on the job is no longer a reason to quit, but now it is an opportunity to show your ability to perform in the toughest of circumstances.

In your efforts to make changes, you will work hard to overcome obstacles, and it will feel as if nobody cares - and the truth is, at times, nobody will. But you must remember that God is always watching and listening. He's watching when you press forward and he's watching when you give up. He's listening when you speak well and he's listening when you speak woe.

I remember a time, when I first became a Pastor. I had been given an opportunity to appear on a Christian television network. While in the makeup room preparing to go on, I had the opportunity to speak with another Pastor named Mark Chironna. I didn't know who he was at the time, but I learned that night that Mark Chironna is one of the most well known and sought after preachers in the world; and for good reason. His gift for ministry is second to none. Right there in the makeup room he began to minister to me. He didn't know me; I hadn't even spoken to him, but somehow he knew that I was a new Pastor struggling with the growth of my church...or the lack thereof. The words he shared with me were very profound and have stuck with me for years. He encouraged me to "stop preaching to the people and preach to the Lord"! He said "the membership that I sought after was not in the seats but it was in my loins, and the more that I preached to God the more he would take what was inside of me and use it to fill the seats. My assignment at that point in my ministry was to learn to make God my audience. Once I learned to do this I would attract audiences that the building could not hold". I never made it on the show that night (I will tell you more about that experience a little later), but I believe that the Lord sent me there that night to hear those words.

The point in what Pastor Chironna shared with me was this: *People are going to let you down and life is going to come against you, but only God can promote you - so he has to be the one that you seek to impress above all others*. The bible tells us **"promotion does not come from the east, the west or the south, but God is the judge: he puts down one, and sets up another (Psalm 75:6&7, KJV)**. Notice the scripture only references the east, west and south. It never mentions the north; because the north represents a high place. Anytime you seek something from the north you are always looking or moving in an upward direction. You know what else the north represents? Cold temperatures! Change comes through upward movement and upward thinking, even when things around you are cold and uncomfortable. Don't cheat yourself out of change because you are afraid to go higher. Don't cheat yourself out of change because you are afraid of cold temperatures. You will have to climb. The world will become cold toward you, but you must continue to seek those things which are above.

One of the ways to keep climbing and moving through the chill in the air is to continuously tell yourself that you deserve more! You have to take on the mentality and even speak the words, "I was promised more, and the only thing keeping me from having my promise is me". I know that there are things in your way and things working against you, but you must believe that these things cannot stop you. _The only thing able to keep you from achieving the changes that you seek is **you**_. Once you recognize this, you must acknowledge it. You must take accountability and be able to tell yourself that you continue to be the only person standing in my own way. Remember this statement: _"wherever you place the blame is where you place the power. Whoever is held accountable also holds the keys"_. When you say that you can't change because of this person or that thing, you have now given that person or that thing the power over your ability to change. If you truly want change you must take back that power. The way to do this is be accountable for everything in your life that needs to change. You must continue to tell yourself "the change that I seek is alive within me, and every day I will remind myself "if I don't change, I am cheating myself out of everything I have been promised"! _Remember, when it comes to change, the "I's" have it_!

Challenged to Change

My friend, the time has come again to lay down this book and do a little self examination. In this chapter I highlighted 4 methods that will aid you bringing change to your life. Now I challenge you to do a 4 -part exercise concerning these 4 methods.

- ❖ Think of the things that you desire to change in your life, and then write down the things that you believe you must do continuously to maintain or enhance that change once it comes to pass. God will not give you anything that you have not prepared yourself to handle. I challenge you to consider your next steps beyond the changes you are expecting to make. I am writing this book, Change or Die, but I already know the titles of my next 2 books. I already have material recorded for them. I believe that this book will change my life along with yours, and I am ready to parlay that change into an even greater change. I challenge you to get ready for the same.

❖ Next, I'd like for you to think on the things that you need to change and write down every negative impact those things are having on your life. Sometimes, we indulge in things for so long that we become numb to the fact that those things are killing us - not just physically, but also killing our hopes, dreams, promises and abilities. My hope is that writing down the negatives in your life will cause you to become fed up and motivate you to change. If you are already fed up and frustrated my hope is that writing these things out will fuel those feelings even more! Remember, you will not maintain any change that your heart is not fully committed to. Nothing will drive you to commit to change more than having to face the burdens that your lack of changed has put on your shoulders.

❖ Next, I'd like for you to write down the names of the people you hold most dear. Next to each name, write out three things that you would most like to do for each one of them. After you write every desire for every person, go back to the top and began to circle every one of those things that you are able to do today. Having to come face to face with the things that you cannot do for the people you love may be tough, but don't be discouraged. Use this list to inspire you to make the necessary changes, so that one day you can draw circles around everything on that list.

- ❖ Lastly, I'd like for you to write down your own name. Underneath it, write out at least 5 things that you believe your change will bring to your life. When writing these things be sure to make them as detailed as possible. For example, you may believe that your change will bring you peace. That's great, but you cannot stop there. Give details…write out what area of your life you are seeking peace, and exactly how you expect this peace to come about. If you believe that your change will put you in position to purchase a new house, write it down and give details. Write down the number of bedrooms and bathrooms, the design of the kitchen; write about the indoor gymnasium and the indoor pool! You

must write the details, because details add excitement and motivation! Once you've done this, I ask that you then do something very important...crumble up that paper and throw it in the trash can! Why would I have you do this? If you take the time to write out your expectations with full details, I can almost guarantee that you will be filled with incredible excitement and expectation. If you are not serious about change, crumbling up that paper won't make you feel anything; but if you are really serious about change crumbling up that paper will make you feel like you are cheating yourself. It will cause you to reflect on the things that you are missing out on, the things that you should already have, and could still obtain if you just began to make changes. If you cannot bring yourself to crumble up that paper, or if you crumble the paper but cannot bring yourself to throw it away, you are on the right track! Take that paper and prayer over it daily! Or begin a journal where you write out what you desire and the steps you are taking to get there on a daily basis. This is something that should only be shared with God. Sure he already knows what you desire, but you must remember, writing a vision makes it plain, but speaking a vision gives it life **(Habakkuk 2:2 KJV, Romans 4:17 KJV)**!

Take a little time, do this exercise, and once your mentality has shifted from "how can I change" to "how can I afford not to change", come back and talk to me more in the next chapter!

Chapter 13

The Ability to Change

Having covered the 4 influences of change I am sure you can relate to them all. You think about changing your life all of time. You are fed with your place in life. You are concerned about making the people closest to you proud. You feel as if you have cheated yourself out of so many of the good things that life has to offer. So if you've already found these things within yourself, I am sure you are asking the question "why haven't I been able to change before now". Let's go back to Romans 7:8, but this time in the

Message Bible. I believe this version will provide a clearer answer to our question.

Don't Get Comfortable!

Romans 7:8-12 (MSG) - *Don't you remember how it was? I do, perfectly well. The law code started out as an excellent piece of work. What happened though was that sin found a way to pervert the command into a temptation, making a piece of "forbidden fruit" out of it. The law code, instead of being used to guide me, was used to seduce me…*

The law code is the knowledge of good. When Paul talks about the law code he is saying that he knew what was right, but he did not do what was right. The reason for this, according to Paul, is that sin found a way to pervert the command into a temptation. He believes that the knowledge of good that was supposed to guide him was used to seduce him. The bible says that we can be changed by the renewing of our minds, but how does change work if I already know what is right? How do I approach change when my mind does not need to be renewed but my actions do not line up with what I know to be right? <u>Could it be that you have allowed yourself to become comfortable</u>

with what you know and that comfort level has fooled you into believing that you cannot be fooled?

As a Pastor, I teach believers to recognize the tricks of Satan. One of his most used tactics is to get you to feel comfortable with wrong doing. Think about how he fooled Eve in the Garden of Eden. He never forced the forbidden fruit into her hand, but he talked to her calmly and confidently, and was able to convince her that she would actually be better off by doing the opposite of what she knew to be right.

This is how Satan works; we expect him to attempt to cause us harm when in fact his most effective plan for disrupting our lives is to convince us to do harm to ourselves. Even if you attend church, study the scriptures, treat people kindly, and have high moral standards; you are not exempt from Satan's plans. He will use your praise, your biblical knowledge, your kindness, even the improvements that you've already made in your life to convince you that you do not need to make any more changes.

In Romans 7:8-12 (MSG), Paul speaks of the things that are supposed to guide us being used to seduce us. The seduction takes place when we become comfortable with our own goodness. The enemy will convince you or trick you into believing that because you are religious, or because you are a good person, or because you are not as bad as the person down the street, you do not have to worry about falling into certain traps. *In order to achieve change, you must never be so focused on your own goodness that you do not concern yourself with the things within you that may not be beneficial to your future*. You must understand that the enemy is counting on you to be comfortable with who you are, because comfortable people are not guarded, and when your guard is down you become an easy target.

Faith vs. Comfort

You may be asking "how can Satan's tricks work on me when I have so much faith"? **You must remember that change takes more than just faith, it also takes work; "faith without works is dead" (James 2:20, KJV).** *When the* *enemy can't shake your faith, he will attempt to trouble your work*.

Many of us have faith, but you must be careful not to allow your faith in a certain thing to extend far beyond the work that you are putting into it. If your work is lacking, I can say with confidence, it is in some way attributed to the involvement of Satan. It may not be that he has done any physical or spiritual damage to what you are trying to achieve; but he has simply made you feel comfortable being who you are and where you are. If you were to go to your Google search engine and type in the words "comfort is the enemy of…" Google will automatically complete your sentence with 3 word options; *progress, growth* and *abundance*. If you research the "enemies of change" you will find *complacency, excuses, discouragement, anxiety, disruptions,* and *waiting!* Satan is calling you to the side of comfort; God is calling you to the side of change, which one sounds like the winning side to you?

Use Your Faith Wisely

Romans 7:8-12 (MSG) -Without all the paraphernalia of the law code, sin looked pretty dull and lifeless, and I went along without paying much attention to it. But once sin got its hands on the law code and decked itself out in all that finery, I was fooled, and fell for it. The very command that was supposed to guide me into life was cleverly used to trip me up, throwing me headlong. So sin was plenty alive, and I was stone dead.

Have you ever looked at a certain situation and wondered; "How did I get here"? You thought there was no way you could fall into such a messy place, yet there you were. You were not inaccurate in your faith, but Satan somehow found away to take what you were fighting against and made it look harmless. You fell for it! You were fooled. I believe we've all been there. *As you pursue change you must be mindful that it is very possible to allow your faith to negatively impact your clear thinking*! You will face situations that are beyond your ability, and you will tell yourself that you can handle it. Even worse, you will be so bold in your faith that you will convince yourself that you are above certain struggles. You must remember that having faith does not make you exempt for using wisdom.

Faith also does not mean that you are exempt from the penalties of not using wisdom.

It is very possible for a person to believe God to move according to their own desires, even when God has no intention to do so. *Why would God allow us to believe him for something that he is not willing to do?* When it comes to God you can have everything you desire, but only when you are prepared. The bible says that **"no good thing will he withhold from them that walk uprightly" (Ps 84:11, KJV)**! Most people remember the beginning of that scripture but often forget the end. You can have whatever you ask, but wisdom will tell you that you cannot have it in any state of being!

Remember, it was this same Paul that declared that the Lord put a thorn in his side, to buffet him, to bother him, to push him back to God continuously. God knew that without that thorn Paul would become overly confident in **his faith** and begin to abandon wisdom. God knew that Paul would eventually begin to think so highly of himself that he would start to believe that he was beyond reproach and enhancement.

Isn't it amazing - the thought that faith could actually work against you if it is not properly utilized. Well believe it or not it can! You must remember that even though faith is you're most essential asset it is only the beginning of the process. After you believe you must think, work and move toward what you believe in. You must not allow faith to make you stubborn and stagnant...standing in one spot looking for God to deliver your blessings to your door step. The bible tells us "without faith *it is* impossible to please *Him,* for he who comes to God must believe that He is, and *that* He is a rewarder of those who diligently **seek** Him" (Heb 11:6, NKJV)! To seek means to means to search, to hunt, to go out and attempt to find! Faith tells you it's yours, wisdom tells you how to go after it. Having one without the other will do you no good.

Be Careful of the Sin Within

Romans 7:13 (MSG) - *I can already hear your next question: "Does that mean I can't even trust what is good [that is, the law]? Is good just as dangerous as evil?" No again! Sin simply did what sin is so famous for doing: using the good as a cover to tempt me to do what would finally destroy me. By hiding within God's good commandment, sin did far more mischief than it could ever have accomplished on its own.*

"By hiding within God's good commandment, sin does far more mischief than it could have ever accomplished on its own". *If you want to change you must recognize when something or someone is a hindrance to the will of God for your life! Not just any kind of hindrance, but a smiling, laughing, nice, sweet, helpful, kind, stress free hindrance*! This scripture highlights an enemy that is hiding in the promises of God. You must understand this is not the enemy that tells you that you **can't** do a certain thing, because those are the people that will fuel you! This scripture speaks of the enemy that tells you that you can make it in your face and then calls you a fool behind your back! This is the enemy that tells you that they are praying for you, but secretly wishes that your plan will blow up in your face. It's the devil hiding within the details of your promise that will do the most damage. *If you want to change, you must know that the enemy is lying right in the midst of God's plan; he is a key contributor to where God is trying to take you. You must understand that the enemy is supposed to be there, but have no fear because he can't stop your progress.*

Remember, you can't be like Jesus if you never experience a Judas. A Judas is someone or something that will walk with you step by step, stick close to you as if they are on your side; and then suddenly turn on you. If you notice with Jesus' dealings with Judas, Jesus was never surprised. He even sent Judas to betray him and told him to do it quickly. Unfortunately Jesus knew that even "His" very presence would not change the nature of Judas, so instead of doing away with him he uses him to bring about his own greatness. *If you want change, you must plan to utilize the bad the same as you plan to utilize the good. You must know that everything and everyone around you is not for you, and every situation is not naturally designed to work in your favor*. Knowing this will give you the ability to laugh, brush off your shoulders and keep moving forward when the ugly truth comes to light. Always remember: *your troubles are just as much a part of the plan as your triumph*! All things work together for the good (Romans 8:28, KJV). Bad things, ugly things, strange things, frustrating things, and things that make no sense at all; if you love the Lord and trust that you have been called according to **his purpose,** even the negative things are working together for your good!

Challenged to Change

Within this chapter I have attempted to explain that there are always challenges to "change" that we just don't see. You cannot properly deal with an issue if you do not recognize an issue. The enemy is smooth and slick; his devices are deceptive and his tenacity is ferocious. He will come at you in ways that are both familiar and unfamiliar so you must have your natural and spiritual wits about you at all times. I challenge you to take a few moments, lay down this book and pray. Pray for God to help you to recognize the enemy in every form and fashion; even the things and people that appear to be harmless. Ask him to help you to see, hear, feel, and notice even the slightest act, the shortest word, the softest touch, and the quickest glance. It is only through prayer that you will be able to detect and discern those things that are good and those that are evil, and once you detect them you will know how to utilize them for your benefit. Take a little time, and pray for these abilities and then come back and talk to me more in the next chapter.

Chapter 14

Change Takes Confidence

A Confident Spirit

A few years ago I remember tuning into one of the more popular Christian television stations; it just so happened they were having a seasonal revival. During this revival some of the most powerful and popular people in gospel were slated to appear. One after the other, mega church pastors, bishops, award winning gospel singers; the show had it all. One speaker in particular caught my attention because he began to spout off scripture after scripture, almost at a rapid pace. As a preacher myself you would think that seeing this would take me to a place of marvel and appreciation, but it actually brought something totally different to mind. Hearing these scriptures spoken with such ease and confidence caused me to reexamine myself. I know my bible but after hearing this person I began to think to myself "maybe I need to step my game up, because I don't know the bible as well as I should". My thoughts quickly began to go from examining myself to second guessing myself. I began to think that maybe I am not as anointed or as prepared as I think I am.

Soon after this I had been given the privilege of being a regular guest on the same television station. One particular night I showed up to do the show that I was a part of, but that night they were taping another revival show. I was nervous, but excited, and ready to go out there and give the people all that I had; but I never made it to the set that night. The decision was made to utilize everyone from our show except for me. It hurt, but I'm strong, and I couldn't let them see that I had been let down. So I stayed at the studio, ate the delicious foods, and watched my show mates go forth on the monitor in the green room. I congratulated them when they were done, and then I left. After that experience I began to think that maybe I was out of my league. Maybe I had been right to second guess myself, and being passed over was God's way of providing validation. It had to be God, in his role as father that took me back to the conversation I had with Pastor Mark Chironna earlier that evening (this is the conversation I shared with you earlier). God let me know that I was there that night to be ministered to, not to minister. God also let me know that he was proud of me for handling the situation the way that I did. He was testing me to see how I would react to this tough situation. Not storming out and staying to congratulate my peers showed that **my spirit** had not been shaken, even though my feelings had been hurt.

1 John chapter 4 says "believe not every spirit but test it whether they are of God" (KJV). Many of us have good spirits and bad flesh. Bad flesh causes us to have bad habits, bad attitudes, bad tempers, bad relationships, and to make bad decisions. Let me encourage you by saying that even with all those short comings, you still have the advantage. Remember, the bible tells us that man judges the outward appearance (the flesh), but God judges the spirit! We should really appreciate God for that, because there are times in all of our lives when we can truly say that the only thing good about us is what we have in spirits. Our flesh can't always be trusted, our relationships are sometimes shaky, and our habits are not always the best; but I believe that each and every one of us has something good within our spirits. *If you are going to change for the better your focus has to be on what you have in your spirit. Not what you have in your hands or in material possessions; the source of your change must come from what you have within*.

Confidence in Spite Of

There is an article found at www.charismamag.com. The article is titled "10 Keys to Move to the Next Spiritual Level", written by Naomi Dowdy. As you take this journey of change I strongly suggest that you read this article...after completing my book of course. Ms Dowdy believes that the first step in moving to the next level in God is to "be convinced of the call". Within this step she explains that "when God begins to take you through the process of change, you must make sure you are absolutely convinced of His call on your life and secure in His purpose as He has revealed them to you". She goes on to explain "when you know that God Himself has called you, nothing can convince you otherwise". You know in your heart that you have clearly perceived God's destiny for your life. You can hear: "This is God's plan and purpose for me".

Your present circumstances won't always resemble or give evidence of God's purpose. Just because God purposed you to be rich does not mean that you won't see any financial hardships. Just because God has purposed good health and long life for you does not mean that you will never face illness. Just because God has purposed success for you does not mean that you will never experience failure. In fact, you will find that God will often use the opposite of what he promised to bring about his purpose for your life! Don't believe me? I challenge you to read the story of Joseph in the book of Genesis.

In the beginning God made a promise to Joseph, that he would be greater than all of his brothers. The revealing of this promise caused Joseph to immediately be thrown into a pit and then sold into slavery. While enslaved he was falsely accused of rape and thrown in prison. While in prison he aided a cellmate in gaining his freedom. Once free that cellmate forgot his promise to help to free Joseph. It took years for Joseph to be released; but once he was released Joseph soon became a ruler. AFTER being enslaved, imprisoned, lied on, forgotten, and hated. God promised Joseph prominence in the beginning, but he never told him that the way to his prominence was by going through the pit, the plantation and the prison. The greatest thing about the story of Joseph is that no matter what physical environment he was in, he still operated according to what was in his spirit. His promise was to be great among men, so he internalized it and secured it in his heart. When he was a slave he became the head of his master's house. When he was a prisoner he became the leader of the prisoners. When he was called to serve for the King he became the head of all of the king's servants. He never allowed what happened to him externally to change what he was purposed to be on the inside. In every situation, the person that Joseph had been purposed to be always came to the forefront. His confidence in what he had inside never wavered, even when the things happening to him on the outside were unpleasant.

Being rejected for the television show was incredibly hurtful. A studio full of ministers, a television show filled with preachers and I was the only one who was told "no thank you". Just like Joseph I had been rejected by my peers. It hit me hard, but I didn't allow it to kill my confidence. I continued to believe, as I still believe today, that there is somebody out there who needs my gift! There is a platform out there that will welcome what I bring to the stage. There is an audience, a church, a stadium, and an arena full of people that are waiting to hear "thus saith the Lord" through me; even if those people don't know it yet. Having a gift that is rejected, ignored or unappreciated by others can drive you crazy if you let it. It can cause you to have feelings or commit actions that are contrary to the will of God and his plan for your life. This is why you must stick to what you have in your spirit, no matter what comes against you. *If you're going to change you have to change what you allow to impact and influence you. You have to be like a tree, planted and rooted in what you feel in your spirit. You have to take on the mentality of Joseph, and make up in your mind that you will be great no matter where life puts you*!

Confidence in God's Timing

I shared my experience with you hoping to encourage you when your situation doesn't line up with your promise. When my gift was ignored, I stayed right there. I shook hands and congratulated those that had been chosen ahead of me. I could have stormed out. I could have gone on social media and blasted everyone in that studio that night, but no; I stayed, I watched and I congratulated. Why? Because I recognized something very important, "*I have the gifting, but God has the timing*"! If God wanted me on that show I would have been up there, front and center. Man would not have been able to stop it; but He chose not to afford me that opportunity at that time. It still didn't change what he put inside of me. It still didn't change what I had the capability to do. As a matter of fact, not only did it not stop me but it fueled me. My thinking became "this opportunity was not mine, but my opportunity will come! When my time does come, I'm going to do my best to preach until the light bulbs pop, the phone lines explode and the internet breaks! I am going to bring every bit of anointing that I have in me and use it to preach until the power of God sets the stage on fire"! I know that may not be a politically correct comment for a preacher, but hey....so what. <u>Nobody tells you how to wallow in pity, so don't allow anyone to dictate how you pursue after glory</u>! You have to find a way to push yourself! You have to find a way to settle your setbacks in your spirit! You have to find a way to smile and be glad for the people in front of you! The way that I am able to do this is to think to myself "I want them to achieve and obtain everything that God has for them, because when God finally releases me I am going after everything, full speed ahead! I do not plan to leave any blessing with my name attached to it unclaimed! I am going to do it all, I'm going to take them all; I am going to get them all! Every opportunity! Every door opened! Every person that wants to join my church! Every media outlet that shows interest in my book! I want it all, and I will have it all! So will you, if you believe!

Humility vs. Lack of Confidence

My friend, please don't think that this is strange talk just because I am a Pastor. Trust me, I am very humble, and I am fully aware that the meek shall inherit the earth (Mathew 5:5); but you must understand that humility and lack of confidence are not the same things. There are loud, boisterous people who have no confidence in themselves. They talk loud and do flamboyant things attempting to draw the attention and the approval of others, all because they do not have the confidence to approve of themselves. There are preachers who do this as well. The only place they are big or important is on the pulpit, so they attempt to stay on the pulpit every chance they get. Being humble has nothing to do with not showing confidence. If you don't believe me let's take a look at David.

While living with his father David's responsibility was to tend to the sheep. He was a humble man until he heard the giant "Goliath" mocking God and God's people. Something about this giant striking fear in the hearts of Godly men caused David to stand up and speak up. When David volunteered to fight the giant, King Saul attempted to place his armor on David. Feeling weighed down, David tells the King that he cannot fight with it on; all he needed was his slingshot and a few stones. When Saul questioned David as to how he believed he could defeat the giant, David revealed to him that a lion had come and stolen one of his father's sheep, and then a bear came and stole another sheep. David chased them both down, and snatched back the sheep. When those animals rose up against him he struck them both in the head and killed them. After telling Saul this, he let it be known **with confidence** that God had given him those victories, and then **with humility** he says that the same God would give him victory over Goliath. David was pumped, he was ready, he was confident, he was sure that he would win the fight; not because of his own abilities, but because of what he believed the power of God could do through him! God never cursed David for standing up and speaking out, in fact, I believe that David's confidence pleased God. In order for the Israelites to defeat the giant, God needed one who was not afraid to face the giant! In David, God found a man after His own heart (Samuel 13:14)...the heart of a champion!

If you want to see change take place in your life you must take on the spirit of David! Everyone talks about victory but **very few** relish the opportunity to stand in the ring and face their giants head on! You have to be one of the few! Change does not come just by having a desire to win; change comes when you develop a desire to fight! Being willing to fight means that you are willing to get hit and keep coming back! God seeks confident people. He seeks people that will look a giant thing in the eye and say to it "you are going down"! He looks for people who can take a whipping and still look their punisher in the face and declare **"you have no power over me" (John 19:11, KJV)**! He's looking for someone to stopping telling Him what they can't do, but instead look at your obstacle and declare that you can and will do all things through **Him (Philippians 4:13, KJV)**! *If you want real change you must have confidence in God, you must have confidence in what you can do through God, and you must have confidence in how far you can go with God*!

Proverbs 3:26 says it perfectly: "for the Lord will be your confidence and will keep your foot from being caught" (NKJV)! Being caught means to be stuck in one place against your own will; unable to change where you are. There are so many scriptures on Godly confidence, I'd never finish this chapter if I began to elaborate on them all, but none of them will mean anything to you if you do not attempt to gain Godly confidence for yourself! So here we go again...

Challenged to Change

I challenge you to put down your book and speak confidence over yourself! Take a few moments, open your mouth and declare out loud *"I want it all! I'm going to get it all! All things are working together for my good! I can do all things through Christ"*! Declare it, and be specific! Say what it is that you can do, achieve, or become! Speak it out loud! Speak so that every demonic force around you can hear it! Speak it so that God knows you are not afraid to speak it! If you have to say it more than once I challenge you to do that! The ability to exercise Godly confidence is essential in your process of change. Do not move on to the next chapter until you feel your confidence growing and getting stronger!

Chapter 15

It Is Really Going To Happen This Time

No Matter How Unbelievable It Sounds

The word of God requires us to believe in a God that is invisible, to feel things that are physically intangible, to overcome obstacles that are immovable, and to claim victory that appears impossible. Ironically, these are also characteristics of mental illness; seeing what's not there, feeling what's not there, and believing what's not there. With the characteristics of faith and insanity being so similar, your spirit is really the only thing you can use to determine God's true instructions. If you allow your spirit to be filled with anything but faith, expectancy, and confidence you may receive a word from God and still dismiss it because it sounds too crazy. You have to pray for the Lord to protect and strengthen your spirit, because you can't risk missing out on your word thinking that it's too crazy to become reality.

If you've ever thought that a word for your life was a little too unbelievable to be real, you are not alone. There was a woman named Sarah who felt exactly what you feel now. In the book of **Genesis, chapter 18 (KJV)**, the bible says that men of God came to Abraham and told him that his wife Sarah was finally going to have the child that she had been promised and desperately wanted for almost 25 years. Sarah over heard them speaking and she laughed. She finally receives the word she has been waiting for, and she laughs because she no longer believes. Sarah is now 89 years old! God made her a promise 24 years prior. Had Sarah received this news in years past she would have been shouting in the streets, but when she looks at the present state of her life, this thing coming to pass just sounds too unbelievable.

Heard That Before

I wonder if you have ever been where Sarah was. You've heard in your spirit that God is going to pay your bills, heal your body, give you what you've spent years believing him for; and instead of becoming excited, you have an attitude of "heard that before". You feel that you've been let down too many times in the past, and now you are unable to take these promises seriously. Sarah felt this way upon hearing that her promise was coming to pass. Instead of being filled with excitement and expectation, she became filled with sarcasm and laughter. When I studied this scripture, I noticed that her laughter was about more than just her ability to conceive a child. As Sarah laughed, the bible says she wonders within her "now, after I have grown old, shall I have **pleasure**". The men of God says that she is going to have a baby, but Sarah isn't thinking about having a baby, she's already let go of that possibility; instead her thinking is "shall I have pleasure". Sarah just wants to experience good feelings again. How could she expect to be happy about the promise when she doesn't feel the same about the promise anymore? She is no longer excited about it, it doesn't move her anymore; she rejects the word by saying that she was too old, but she never openly doubts God. Sarah not questioning the abilities of God lets me know that she still has faith, but in questioning her own abilities, she tells me that she has lost confidence. Sarah's lack of confidence came from her knowledge of her present circumstances.

My friend, have you ever been in a place like Sarah. Where you said I have faith but I've just lost confidence. I can guarantee your lack of confidence is also based on your present circumstances. You feel that money is small, time has been wasted, your surroundings are filled with unsuccessful people, and your past is filled with unsuccessful attempts to change your life for the better. Have you ever wondered why, when you had resources, confidence, and energy; you couldn't hear the Lord's voice? But now that you are discouraged and have very little confidence, God is sending a word? God had to wait until you realized that you couldn't help yourself. He needed to hear you acknowledge that you were nothing on your own. He needed to wait until you knew that what you were praying for was impossible without him! 10 years ago you may not have appreciated it, 20 years ago you would have taken the credit for it, but now that everything at your disposal has dried up, this blessing will establish a greater faith within you than you've ever had before"! Think about it...anyone can have a child in their 20's and 30's, but imagine the confidence of a man that can make a baby at age 100, and a woman who can carry and deliver a baby at the age of 90! Anyone can believe God for 2 years, or maybe 5 years; but to believe God for a promise that takes 25 years to fulfill is faith that cannot be denied!

God's reason for giving Abraham and Sarah a child so late in age, and taking 25 years to fulfill this promise was His way of showing them that no matter what they were dealing with they **could** still have their promise, and no matter how long it took God **would** still honor his word! If you want to experience the change that you seek you are going to have to take on the same belief! Sarah's age was not her issue. It was everything that came with her age that caused her to believe that her time had passed. God had to show her the same thing he is attempting to show you. <u>No matter what life has done to you, you still have the power and ability to conceive, carry, labor and deliver what God has promised you! You must also believe that this time is "the time"</u>. Right before God finally changed Sarah and Abraham's life, he sent them a messenger to alert them that their time had finally come. Through this book God is using me in the same manner; as your messenger to tell you that your time has finally come! When Sarah laughed the messengers became upset, because her laughter showed that she lacked faith. She is 90 years old and 9 months away from her life being changed for the better; this was not the time for doubt!

My friend, I cannot say that you are 9 months away from experiencing your change, but I can say with confidence that you are closer than you've ever been in your life! God has sent me to give you the word that this is your time and your season, and the greatest change of your life is at hand; but you still have a little while to go. Now is the time that your faith must be stronger than it has ever been! There is no room for games, doubt, or wavering. During this period leading to your change, you must treat it the same as Sarah does after receiving her word. You must conceive it, you must carry it, you must labor, and you must deliver!

Challenged to Change

The time has come to put down the book yet again, and this time I challenge you to speak against the spirit of unbelief! You are only human, and the fact that you have been disappointed in the past is going to make this process of change even tougher. You must believe that this time is "your time", and the only way to give life to that belief is to open your mouth and declare it! I challenge you to do that now. Lift your voice and speak against doubt. Open your mouth and declare that no matter what has or has not happened at this point in your life, you **can** still do it, and God **will** still do it, through you! **You will conceive the change! You will carry the change! You will labor through the change! You will deliver the change!** Take a few minutes and speak those words over yourself; make it a personal declaration that you recite on a daily basis! Put those words into the atmosphere, and then come back and let's talk more in part 4!

CHANGE or DIE
PART 4
THE PROCESS OF CHANGE

Chapter 16

The Way to Change

Change vs. Changing

I am a business major. I have earned an Associate in General Business, a Bachelors of Business Administration, and a Masters in Business Management. In pursuing these degree's, and also working within the corporate structure for several years, I have found that one of the reoccurring messages echoed throughout the business world is the notion that people are resistant to change! An article from business research giant Forbes Magazine, states "*change has an interesting way of affecting people that can often result in resistance. This resistance can range from fairly subtle, such as avoidance or passive aggressive behavior, all the way to outright defiance, hostility, and sabotage".* I'd like to change the perplexity of the conversation by providing a different outlook to these behaviors. I know that I am just a small voice in comparison to Forbes, but working within corporate America and experiencing the behaviors of the individuals first hand has lead me to believe that people **are not** resistant to change. I do however believe that people are resistant to changing.

I believe that everyone in the world has at least three things, three people, three decisions, or three situations we desire to change for the better. Everybody wants "change", but not everybody wants "to change". If I offered you millions of dollars right now, you would take it and celebrate, because it would possibly change everything about your financial situation. But if I told you that I was not going to give you the money, but instead I would give you the tools to be able to make it for yourself your reaction would more than likely be very different. You would probably be interested until you learned that you would have to give up or walk away from things, behaviors or people in order to obtain the millions. Experience has shown me that the minute change becomes tough we have a greater tendency to abandon it. The reason why is simple, we DO want change, we just don't want anyone to attempt to change us! We take a stance that says "change my money, change my job, change the people around me, change everything concerning me or connected to me for the better, but you'd better mind your business the minute you start to sight changes that need to happen within me"!

What we miss when taking that stance is that outward change only takes place after something changes on the inside. If I gave you those millions of dollars and you haven't made any internal changes, within 6 months to 1 year you'd more than likely be back in the same financial state you were in before receiving the money. If you don't change internally more money will only give you opportunities to do more of the same things that you've already been doing. _It doesn't matter what changes around you, if there is no change on the inside, every change on the outside will only be temporary_. Think about your own life; how many job opportunities have you had and lost? How many loans and tax refunds have you had and are still in the same financial position? How many different relationships in your life have ended or been impacted by the same set of circumstances? If you're honest with yourself you will recognize that at least half of those things did not work out because things changed around you but nothing changed within you. Be honest.

Seek

Lack of seeing positive changes take place often causes us to become frustrated with the plan of God for our lives. Why would God's plan frustrate us…because what we see is not what he said and we are not seeing **him** change our realities to mirror your destiny. We want God to send changes our way, and when he doesn't it leads to frustration. I believe this way of thinking is not the reason for our frustrations but it is in fact the source of it. Waiting on God's plan to come together is necessary, but it can become increasing frustrating if you are waiting for it without working toward it. The bible tells us that God is "a rewarder of those who diligently **seek** him". On this walk you must remember that *change is a destination not a* *delivery. Change is sought not sent*. Change is not going to walk into your bedroom and shake you out bed in the morning. Change is not going to just come to you and hand you the keys to success, health and a better way of life. There is a reason why we say that we are **GOING TO "CHANGE"**, because change is an actual place of arrival. In order see change, you are going to have to pursue it! Just looking for it won't get it for you. Just expecting it will not make it appear. Change is not coming to you, but you must go out and get it for yourself!

The Way

John 14:6 (KJV) - Jesus saith unto him, I am the way, the truth, and the life: no man cometh unto the Father, but by me.

Jesus not only declared himself to be the truth and the life, but before both he declared that he was" the way". We all want God's promises, goodness, and everything that we've believed him for to be true! We all want the life we feel we have been destined to live! But how can we expect the truth and desire the life without seeking the way? They all come together; you can't have the second or the third portion without seeking after the first. The truth and the life will come, but first you must seek the way! And my friend, allow me to tell you that the way is not always pleasant. The way is filled with tears, heart break, pain, and even betrayal. Just look at Jesus! He is the savior of the world, but his way was filled with phony friends, stubborn followers, unbelievers, and people who sought to kill him for no reason at all. Jesus was gifted from birth, but the book of Luke tells us that after he stayed behind in Jerusalem to teach in a temple at 12 years old he became subject to his parents until he was 30 years old. All of those great miracles you read about from Jesus happened within a 3 year time span; prior to that he spent 18 years in a holding pattern. During that time he lost his father, he lived in Nazareth (which was equivalent to modern day ghetto), and the bible tells us **"he was at all points tempted as we are, but was without sin" (Hebrews 4:15, KVJ)**. Jesus' destination was great, but his path was not one to envy. At any point he had the choice to walk away. At any time he could have decided that the reward wasn't worth the head ache and been carried back to his rightful place in Heaven. Thankful for us Jesus did not take advantage of this opportunity. Instead he stayed his course with an understanding that his hard time was just the way to get to the good times. He understood that in between "the way" and "the life" was the truth, and the truth was that his God was not a man that he should lie, nor the son of man that he should repent! If God said that something great was coming out of everything he had allowed Jesus to go through, no matter how challenging the circumstances, somehow some way it was going to happen!

Jesus pressed through "the way", he walked in "the way", but he believed in "the truth" and kept his focus on "the life". Every word that proceeds out of the mouth of God is truth; and everything that you believe God has spoken over your life is truth. If by chance you believe in something that God really did not promise, don't worry, what you believe now will lead you to the truth! God is not the author of confusion, so just in case you are confused, which is allowed because you are only human, your faith and desire for God's truth will lead you in the right direction! God's word **is** true, and the righteous, successful, sin free life that you see in your spirit is the life that he wants for you; but you cannot have the truth and the life and forsake the way. So, just in case you are in a place where you know your truth and you can see your life, but you're struggling with the way, I have yet another challenge for you!

Challenged to Change

I challenge you to make these 2 very important requests of the Lord...

- ❖ "Have your way"!
- ❖ "Show me your way"!

I challenge you, just for a few moments, to repeat those words! Repeat them until you believe that God believes you! Repeat them until you mean them! Repeat them until you receive an answer! This is a must! *If you want to see change take place in your life you must be willing to seek God for the path that you must walk*. You've got a big vision! In order to achieve it you are going to need people and resources that you have no way of knowing how to reach or obtain yourself. You need a path, you need the way, and only God has what you need! So you have to do this! You have the let him know that you need what he has and the only way that God is going to give it to you is if you ask and obey! That's why I'm telling you to repeat these words. Don't just say them but repeat them. Repeat them until you get them in your mind and your spirit. Repeat them until you're willing to abide by them. Take some time, and deal with this and then come back and talk to me in the next chapter.

Chapter 17

Change Is In The Opposite Direction!

Get Up, Turnaround and Move!

Waiting on God is great, it's biblical, it's necessary, but we sometimes we take it too literally. We don't see anything, we don't feel anything, we don't know what to do next, so we just sit down and take up residence where we are. Our thought process is *"Lord I'll just be here until you come for me"*, but the Lord is omnipresent, which means that in the low place, the empty place, even in the dead place he's right there with you! So then the question becomes *"Lord if you're here with me why aren't you doing anything for me"?* His reply is *"I'm not here to fix this; I'm here to tell you to get up, turnaround and move away from this"*! <u>If you want to experience change you must ensure that you are not in a place where God does not want you to be! As long as you stay where you are things will never change</u>.

1 Kings Chapter 19 tells of how Elijah stood for God, and won a great victory. His reward for this victory was a threat of death from Queen Jezebel. Elijah became fearful and retreated until he finally reached Horeb, the mountain of God. Once in the mountain he went into a cave to hide and also to sulk and to wallow due to his present circumstances. The bible says that during his retreat an angel gave him food which gave him incredible strength, but he used that strength to run away from his calling. God allowed him to run to the mountain. But once he reached the mountain, while hiding in a cave, the Lord asked him "what are you doing here". God does not stop Elijah from going, but he challenges Elijah once he's there. He tells

Elijah to come out of the cave and stand in his presence, and then he asks him again "what are you doing here". There are three things you need to pick up from this story...

- ❖ **God will give you strength, but it's up to you to apply it this will.** God strengthen Elijah and instead of using that strength to oppose his enemies he used it to run and hide. _Take a second and ask yourself "what are you using your strength to do"_? Do you use it to find different was to run from your calling? Do you use it to find ways to be seen by people instead of being used by God? Do you use it to fight and argue with people who are trying to help you? _If you're going to change, you're going to need strength, and in most cases we already have the strength that we need, we are just using it in a way that is opposite of it intention_. What are you using your strength to do?

- ❖ **Elijah heard God's voice and stood in his presence, while he hid in the cave.** That lets us know that God is still with him, even while he was not in the place that God would have him to be. Understand something my friend: *God does not operate "out of order".* <u>*It is quite possible that God could be with you and doing nothing more for you than keeping breath in your lungs and food in your stomach; not because he doesn't care, but because he cannot operate for you in the place where your standing*</u>. The only thing he can do is keep you alive until you change your mind and your space. Maybe that's why things aren't changing for you at this time in your life, because your change is set to take place in the valley, but you are hiding in the mountain? <u>*If you want to experience change you must ask yourself "where am I now"? "Am I where God wants me to be or am I where I want to be"*</u>? You'll know the answer by examining what God is doing for you in your present position. If you are doing nothing more than surviving that is a good indication that God is keep you alive, waiting for you to realize you are not in position to receive your promise.

- ❖ **God pushed Elijah to get out of the cave and get to work on his assignment!** God pushed him by simply questioning him and making him explain why he was there. What lead you to this place in your life? What caused you to run away from what and who you were destined to be? God is there in the cave with Elijah, but he was not there to sit with him, he was there to pull him out of it! God did not force him out, God made him come to terms with what lead him to this place. Elijah was disappointed in God. He felt that he was the only one doing God's will and he deserved better than death threats. God gave Elijah a new assignment but not until Elijah came clean about his feelings and what lead him to the place where he was at the present time. Before you can change you must set aside some time and really come to terms with where you are presently. Ask yourself, where was I before I arrived here? Have I done wrong to someone? Has someone done wrong to me? What circumstances, situations or decisions caused me to arrive in this place in my life? If you don't understand how you've gotten to where you are, you'll never understand how to get to where you want to go.

God Wants You!

Understand this, in the scripture Elijah ran for 40 days and 40 nights before he faced his issue. After doing this he went back and reclaimed his position. Had he never faced his issue he could have possibly continued to run in the opposite direction of where he was supposed to be for many more days. I believe that someone reading this book is standing at the same crossroad. You haven't really come to terms with what has taken place in your life and you have been moving in the opposite direction of where God would have you to be. I'm here to warn you: if you don't come to terms with what has already taken place in your life, and really seek to understand why things have turned out the way they have, you could be running from what you are supposed to be for the rest of your life!

Elijah felt that he was the only one doing right and still the only one being punished. You probably feel that way right now. But God let Elijah know that he had 7000 others who had not bowed, meaning he had 7000 others who were faithful to him and had either suffered or were willing to suffer just as Elijah had. That tells me that Elijah was not the only one that God had for this assignment, but he was the only one that God had chosen for this assignment. I believe that as you come to terms with the reasons behind where you are at this point in your life, God will reveal the same thing within you! *You are not his only option for what he has called you to do but you are his only choice*!

You are the person God **wants**! He could have chosen many others but he **wants you**! He **wants you** to fulfill a great assignment! He **wants you** to live a life that many will only dream about! He **wants you** to be his champion, gaining victory over deadly situations! But more than anything he **wants you** to come out of your cave; stop running away from the fight and start running towards it! Races are won by outrunning the opponent not running away from them. God **wants you** to stop hiding and start running in the right direction! Be warned - *the right direction is often a road that leads to tough obstacles and difficult people* – don't focus on that! Romans 8:30 tells us "those he predestined, he also called; those he called he also justified; those he justified, he also glorified"! No matter how difficult the race, if God **wants you** to run it there is nothing but glory for you at the finish line!

Challenged to Change

At this point, I challenge you to take a hard look at your life. Examine where you are now and how you really got here. If it was due to fear acknowledge it, if it is because you allowed people to hold you back acknowledge it, if you've made a poor decision acknowledge it; no matter what it is acknowledge it. Then allow God to tell you about you. Let him tell you the ugly truth; allow him to show you your short comings. God did that for Elijah simply by telling him that he was full of himself; but after God told Elijah this, he gave him an assignment and additional strength to carry it out. Let God read you, be open to his critiques, allow him to reestablish your path and then come back and meet me in the next chapter!

Chapter 18

The Harsh Reality of Change!

Change Costs

If you were to go to the 6th chapter and start reading at the 11th verse of 1 Kings, you would be picking up on a story of a Syrian army who sought to take the life of the prophet Elisha. As they approached Dothan where Elisha was, the bible says that he asked the Lord to make them blind. The Lord makes this army blind, and Elisha tells them that they have come to the wrong place and he leads them to

Samaria. When they arrive at their destination Elisha asks the Lord to give them their sight back. Once they can see again they discover that they are standing at the mercy of the King of Israel. The bible says that when the king sees this enemy at his disposal he asks the prophet Elisha if he could kill them. Elisha says "no, we do not kill prisoners of war. Give them something to eat and let them go home". The King, against his own will and judgment, does as Elisha commands and then sometime later the Syrians return and conquer Israel.

When Israel had a chance to conquer Syria, the king does the right thing and lets them go, but these same people come back later and conquer Samaria, which brings about a famine in the land. The first mind of the King was to kill these people, to do away with them, but he listened to the voice of the Lord spoken through the prophet and he lets them live. My friend, I am not so desperate to get a rave review from you that I would rob you of the truth. I know you want change around you, I believe you're ready for change to happen within you, but you must know this: <u>the very first result of change is always loss</u>. The minute you decide to change you have to be prepared to lose something. People and things that you have grown to depend on – get ready, someone or something is going to leave your life!

Change first results in loss, and with loss comes suffering. You are going to cry sometimes. You are going to wonder if you've made the right choices. You are going to kick yourself for putting yourself in this position. You are going to take hits to your confidence. You are even going to have days where your discomfort becomes so great that you attempt to rationalize giving up on your change! God sent me to tell you to hang in there. If you press forward you will eventually see that a great loss has a way of leading to an even greater gain in God's plan.

Expect the Not So Great

Just as much as you expect the great, you must expect the grief; the key is to **expect it**! Many people miss out on "great outcomes" simply because they did not expect the difficulties that came along with their new path. I recently took place in a panel discussion for Millennials. Some of them expressed that they were turned away from attending church because they had encountered individuals within church who claimed to be righteous but then exhibited behaviors that did not line up with righteousness. My response was this "we must stop expecting to see perfect people within the church. The church is a hospital for those who have spiritual sicknesses. Any kind of sin you find in the world you will more than likely find those who struggle with those same sins within the church. The key is not to allow the short comings of the members to negatively impact the validity of the message. The word of God is always right, even if the people of God are not. No matter what you encounter, your focus must be **his word**".

This same statement applies when you are pursuing change. The change that God has for your life is surrounded by things and people who have the ability to turn you away. The key is to expect them so that you can be prepared to handle them accordingly. God's plan is laced and laden with negativity and difficulty. The reason for this is to force you to lean and depend on him. It is also God's way of preparing you to face the world as a new you! If you cannot handle God's training how will you win a war with the enemy?

You must even expect to see "not so great" things within yourself. Change is not easy; it is fulfilling but not always fun, necessary but not always nice, timely but sometimes tiring. You are not going to always like it or be good at, especially in the beginning. Expect this, and know that God expects it of you. Why do you think the bible says that "His mercies are new every morning"? Because he knows that you are going to make mistakes today. But understand this: mercy is for those who acknowledge pain and struggle, not for those ignore it or run from it.

Now or ~~Never~~ Next!

In the sport of wrestling, if a wrestler finds them self caught in a position they cannot escape all they have to do is waive their hand, pound the mat or shake their head in the "yes" motion. This tells the referee that they cannot handle this position and they need mercy. The referees will not intervene until they see the signal. The wrestler may lose that fight, but they are allowed to come back and fight again – next time better prepared because of what they faced previously. Understand this: *in the beginning of change you are not going to win every day. You are not going to win every fight. You are going to find yourself entangle in situations that you cannot find your way out of.* In God there is no failure, but you are not God. You are going to fail at something eventually. *The key is to stay focused on the fighter in you, **not** the failure in you*! Every champion has lost at some point in their career. What made them a champion is how they responded. They used their setbacks as setups for victory in the next fight! Understand my friend you must live and be striving for victory now! But if you are not able to take full advantage of now, you must prepare yourself to be next; "never" is not an option.

Next is a Gift not as a Promise

God's daily gift to us is mercy. If He blesses you with a new day take advantage of the new mercy. But you must also understand that "mercy" is not "victory"! It simply means that you have another opportunity to obtain victory. You must also understand that tomorrow is not promised, and mercy alone adds no benefit. If you have not learned from your yesterday the mercy you receive today will provide no different result. Use mercy if you need it, but know that as long as you need it you have not won anything. Your gift is mercy, but your goal is victory – never place your gift in front of your goal!

Challenged to Change

This time around I'd like to challenge you with 3 tasks...

- ❖ **Acknowledge your failures and learn from them!** We often give a great deal of our attention to our accomplishments but the source of change lies in our ability to recognize and acknowledge where we've come up short. I said earlier that "all champions have lost at some point in their careers", well allow me to give you an example of what happened when you cannot admit defeat. Back in 2014, Welterweight Boxing Champion Floyd Mayweather Jr faced a young contender by the name of Marcos Maidana. Mayweather won the fight, but had to do so after 12 rounds and a highly contested decision. The fight was so close that one of the judges called it a draw and the other 2 only score Mayweather the winner by a combined 10 points. After the fight Maidana declared that he was in fact the real winner regardless of the decision. Because the fight ended in such a close decision a much anticipated follow-up match was scheduled for September 2014. My wife and I were terribly excited; so much so that we watched hours or pre-fight interviews. I remember telling my wife that Madiana was going to lose. Not because he did not have the strength or the ability to win, but because in every interview he continued to declare that he had won the first fight! In his mind, he was already the winner. He had not come up short the first time around. I was right. Not only did Mayweather win but he score and even more decisive victory than in the first fight. I truly believe that because Madiana could not admit to coming up short the first time he did not prepare to come out ahead the next time. I believe that he felt he needed no improvement. If he went out and performed the same as before he would see a different result. Mayweather on the other hand did prepare. In the second fight he was faster, smart, and more aggressive. He approached the fight has if he had lost the first one and he was determined to ensure that he would not lose this time around. This is what acknowledging failure is supposed to do for you! It is not meant to cause you to weep or wallow, but to motivate you to make the necessary adjustments, so that the next time around you will be faster, smarter and more aggressive in your efforts to obtain the victory! Mayweather changed based on his failures in the first fight, Madiana did not. Mayweather walked away a champion, Madiana did not. Which type of fighter are you? Admit your failures now so that you can walk away a champion next time!

- ❖ **Ask for Mercy!** There is absolutely nothing wrong with admitting that you cannot get out of what you are in. You are in a wrestling match with your past. Your past is bigger than you! It's stronger than you! It's more experienced than you are. At curtain points in your life your past is going to get the better of you. Don't allow it to keep you entangled! Don't allow it to continue to hold you in a position that you cannot shake free of. The Lord is your referee. He's waiting for you to ask for mercy. He won't just give it to you and he won't count you out. But the second you give him the signal he will command the past to release you from its grip! It is perfectly acceptable to ask for mercy as long as you have this understanding: the bible says that God's mercies are new every MORNING! This means that at the start of every day you get a new opportunity to fight! Mercy is only meant for short term recuperation. It is not meant to drag the fight along, weeks, months, years, but if you find yourself needing mercy today you are expected to come back in and take advantage of it in the MORNING! The next day! Right away! Acknowledge your failures; learn from them, and then as quickly as you can get right back in that ring and fight!

- ❖ **Pray to God and declare over yourself "this is the last time I will need Mercy"!** You must remember: Mercy is not Victory! Escape is not outcome! Another chance is not a guarantee! The need for mercy is evidence that you lack strength, knowledge, skill, and the ability to withstand pain. These are not the traits of a winner. Lacking these things will only bring you consistent defeat and will ultimately bring about "demise". The scripture does tell us that *mercy* is new every morning but never forget that morning only comes for those who *make it* through the night! Pray for mercy! Thank God for mercy! But ultimately, when it comes to your change, you don't want to lean on the gift of mercy, you want to stand on your ability to make it!

Chapter 19

Provoked to Change!

If I Change We All Change

This King in our scripture, 2 Kings Chapter 6, wanted to kill the Syrian army when Elisha first brought them to his doorstep, but instead he listened to the voice of the prophet and let them live. This decision shows that he has become a different individual; changing his thinking from punishing his enemies to obeying God even if it means allowing his enemies to walk away. The issue is that these people come back and caused a great famine in his land. The king is already frustrated, but a conversation with a certain women in verses 28 and 29 causes him to snap! This woman says "my king, another woman proposed that we eat my son one day and her son the next. So we boiled my son and ate him, but the next day when I said "kill your son so we can eat him", she hid him". When the king hears this woman's testimony he tore his clothes in an act of outrage and frustration. All he wanted to do was to change - to become a better person - but now his change has brought out the worse in his followers. <u>*Be warned my friend, a positive change within you is going to bring out a negative change within others*</u>. **Be ready, it's going to happen!**

You must remember that your change impacts the people around you, rather they agree to what you are attempting to change or not. When the king made the choice not to do away with the Syrian army he put his entire kingdom at risk, not just himself. When you decide that you are going to began handling things differently in your life, your family, friends and confidants are going to have deal with the fallout of your change - good or bad, like it or not. In dealing with this fallout you are going to have tough conversations and experience personality changes in people that you never would have imagined; but don't be alarmed. This must happen so that you will know where and how to position people in your life. And be mindful of this: <u>where a person is placed in your life should **not only** be based on their willingness to support you, but also their ability to support you</u>. People are sometimes willing but just not emotionally, physically or spiritually able. Do to the level of your commitments and responsibilities, you're willing supporters may be too inexperienced, immature or unavailable to give you what you need. This is why it is terribly important to recognize the effects that your change has on the people around you.

Who Belongs Where

As you progress through change you need to know that the people closest to you are not going to fall apart or lose their heads just because a situation does not go as planned or preferred. You are going to be battling enough with your own decisions, confidence and faith. For that reason it is important, as we have previously discussed, to have people around that will not add more stress to the process. It is not good enough for a person to only behave with decency, strength and level headedness when everything is going well for you. _A person shows you who they really are when times get rough and they are able to maintain or increase their value! If a person is with you they have to know that your change may bring some struggle for them as well_. If they can't hold it together when those struggles take place, you must reevaluate where you place them in your life. Your change will show you who belongs where. Some people will show themselves to be beneficial, others will show you negative qualities that you would have never expected to see from them.

If you do not want to see negative behaviors coming out of the people around you, simply don't make any changes. As long as you don't change, the people around you won't either. But the minute you start saying "no" to the things that you used to say "yes" to; once you start to talk bigger, plan bigger, and move toward bigger things, start watching the people around you closely…someone is going to change for the worse.

You must understand their reactions at first. In all fairness to them, they have known you to have been a certain type of person for a long period of time, and it'll be quite shocking for the people around you to adjust to the "new you". Your prayer has to be that the positive change within you will bring about a positive change within them; especially if you are connected through marriage or blood. Even those relationships have the potential to become rocky or even unhealthy when you began to change. Stay prayed up, keep your eyes and heart open, and by all means, do not allow the negative reactions of people to stop your positive change!

The Pain Underneath

The bible says that when the king ripped his clothes, the people could see that he had on sackcloth underneath his royal garment. I mentioned this a few chapters ago. Kings wore their royal garments as they walked before the people, but sackcloth was worn when a person prayed in mourning or repentance. I am certain that we have all been in a place in life where we wore our royal robes on the outside in an effort to give a sustained or carefree appearance to others. While underneath that manufactured exterior, we were crying and praying because we had no idea what to do about our hidden struggles. We've all struggled with negative feelings brought on by our mistakes or poor decisions, and we just couldn't allow the people around us to see how much those situations affected us. So in an effort to maintain our privacy we wear our regal robes on the outside and our sackcloth underneath. By *"regal robes"* I am referring to smiles and laughter that contain no happiness or joy; works and efforts that contain no confidence or assurance; conversations and interactions with no passion or interest; even displaying extroverted or aggressive behaviors in an effort to cover fears, doubts and insecurities.

Change Clothes

This king became so enraged by the pain underneath that he rips his own outer covering, revealing his true feelings to everyone around him. *In order to achieve change you must understand that a time is coming when what you truly feel will be too much for you to contain*. And though it is imperative that you not *expose* yourself, you must know that a time is coming when you must *reveal* yourself. To be *exposed* means to be uncovered or unprotected, but to be *revealed* means to be shown off, displayed, or unveiled! Anything *"exposed"* is usually brought to the light by one individual in an effort to show the misdeeds or poor behaviors of another. But something *"revealed"* is meant to release a secret that no longer benefits anyone by being tucked away. And understand this: just as the king ripped his outer covering due to his internal pain, the pain associated with your change will lead you to do the same.

As you pursue change, there is going to come a time when <u>hiding will bring about hurting</u>. The in-genuine behaviors that you use to cover your truth will began to squeeze and suffocate you, until you are forced to rip and tear away everything from your life that does not allow you to live and breathe freely. In order to experience the change you seek, you are going to have to do as the king does and essentially "change clothes" - from the beautiful comfortable garments that allow you to fit in, to the ugly uncomfortable garments that cause you to standout. Before the king ripped his garment he was simply pacing back and forth along a wall, going through the motions while still going nowhere. Once those garments were torn his true feelings where revealed, and he become driven to address his situation immediately.

The bible says that when the king heard what these women had done, he made a vow to execute the prophet Elisha. Allow me to say this and understand me very clearly, the king was misguided in his resolution, but commendable in his approach. I know that he made a vow to kill, **which is absolutely wrong**, but what he was really saying…in his misguided way… is "I'm fed up and I'm about to do something about this right now"!

Challenged to Change

My friend, I challenge you to determine within yourself that you are done covering your ugly truth with a beautiful lie. Sometimes, making changes simply means making choices, and at this point *I challenge you to choose*. Will you continue to put on a front for people, going through the motions of your life but never going to the next stage of your life? Or will you rip and tear away everything that does not fit who you are really meant to be and pursue after your destiny with a reckless abandon? The king made the choice and it caused him to move in the right direction...but unfortunately with the wrong intentions. He moved pursuing revenge instead of reward, which caused him to pursue death instead of life. The king made up his mind and then he moved, he never stopped to do what you are about to do, which is to "pray first".

I challenge you now to choose not to conceal your truth any longer, but to reveal it, and then make up your mind to change it. But before you move it is imperative that you seek the Lord concerning your feelings, so that you may ensure that your *positive movements* are filled with *positive motive*. Remember: revenge belongs to God, but rewards are set aside for you. Pray until you are sure that you are pursing only what's yours. Take some time, do this now, and then let's go further into our journey to change.

CHANGE or DIE

PART 5

THE FAITH TO CHANGE

Chapter 20

Changed By Faith

Beware of Broken Faith

In the last chapter, we left discussing the king and the woman, and how they had allowed famine to push them both to make poor decisions. We'll get back to that story shortly but I wanted to examine what really caused them to take a turn for the worse. Yes, famine played a major role in their decision making, but the bigger issue is that they allowed their conditions to cause them to operate in **broken faith**. <u>If you are going to change for the better your</u>

faith can not be broken...ever! You must understand that when it comes to change your faith is the determining factor.

So what is faith? The book of Hebrews, chapter 1 defines faith as being "the substance of things hoped for and the evidence of things not seen". Google defines faith as "complete trust in someone or something"; "strong belief in God or in the doctrines of a religion, based on spiritual apprehension rather than proof". My personal definition would be a bit shorter and to the point. *Faith is complete trust and strong belief in God* **and something**, *based on spiritual apprehension rather than things that we have seen or can prove*. Notice that I said that you must have faith in God and *"something"*.

"Something" would be a word, a promise, a warning, an instruction or even a gift given to you or promised to you by God. That may seem to go without saying, but there are a great many people who have faith in God but do not have faith *in "the things of God"*. If you are going to experience the change that you seek you have got to be different. *It cannot be enough to just know that God is there, but you have to have faith in what he's said in his word, what he's told you personally, what he's promised to bring to pass in your life, and what you feel him doing in the atmosphere*. You have to be able to declare "Lord, I believe in you and every word that you say, every promise that you've made, and every direction that you've given. Even when it doesn't look or feel good, I still have faith that *SOMETHING* bigger, better and greater is in store for my life"!

Believing in God and Looking for Something

I know that it sounds a bit strange to say that you believe in God and "something", because simply saying "something" sounds so unsure. I can imagine that sounding unsure does not sit well with many of us because we feel that we **know** what God is going to do - we're just waiting on him to do it! It is great to have such confidence in God but allow me to pose a few questions for your consideration...

- ❖ What if God is planning to do something bigger than what you think you know?
- ❖ What if your vision is too small?

- ❖ What if your desires are beneath your abilities?
- ❖ When you consider what it is that you "know" God is going to do, you must also consider the question "how do you know"?
- ❖ Is the thing that you believe him for something he described or something you desire? How are sure that you are not confusing God's WILL with your WANTS!

The bible says clearly and without hesitation **"we know not what we should pray for as we ought" (Rom 8:26, KJV)**. So when you read this, and you consider what it is you "*know*", how can you be so sure of what's coming when the bible says that you don't even know what to pray for? I'm not trying to break your faith my friend, but *if you have faith that tells you that God is only going to do what you want, how you want, and when you want, your faith is already broken*. Broken - not in the since of being "smashed to pieces" - but broken in the sense of "not operating properly". Kind of like a car that cuts off every time you stop, but it starts right back up every time you turn the ignition; so you keep driving it, because it may be broken but it still runs. Unfortunately, that scenario describes the faith of a great deal of individuals; *it's running, but it's not working.*

Running Faith vs. Working Faith

Working faith understands that even after you give God your wish list, **which is absolutely OK to do,** you must make room in the end for him to have his way in your life. A person with running faith asks God to give them everything they desire and then they run around looking for it. They run from person to person looking for Mr. or Mrs. Right. They run from idea to idea looking for something that will stick. They run from job to job looking for the one that satisfies their desires. A person with running faith is always *on the run*, but a person with working faith is always *on the move*.

A person with working faith asks God for what they want and then gives God room to operate within his will. *Running faith is in constant pursuit, but working faith is in constant preparation*. Running faith always says "I have to have it", but working faith says "I have to be ready for it"!

Running faith says that this must not be God because it doesn't feel good or sound good, but working faith understands that **his ways are not our ways and his thoughts are not our thoughts (Isaiah 55:8, KJV).**

Believing God for "something" is so important because all of us have experienced God's blessings in a way that we never expected. The outcome may have been what you expected but the process was different; or the process may have been what you expected but the outcome totally blew your mind. Working faith opens your heart and you mind to whatever God wants to do, however God wants to do it. Running faith becomes anxious and impatient when it doesn't recognize the ways of God.

Running Faith Won't Last

Let's take quick look at a story about 2 brothers found in the book of **Genesis, chapter 25 (KJV)**. Their names are Jacob and Esau. Esau, being the older of the two, was entitled to receive a birthright, which would grant him "head of house" status. This gave him authority over his father's estate and a double portion of whatever was passed down. His brother Jacob, however, tricked his father into bestowing the birthright upon him instead of Esau. When Esau returned home to find what had been done he vowed to kill Jacob once their father was dead. Fearing for his life, Jacob **ran** and went to live with his uncle. If you move ahead in the scripture to chapter 32, Jacob is now a man of wealth. He has wives, children, employees, cattle; everything a man could ask for in that time. Then he receives word that his father is dead and his brother is coming to see him.

Out of fear Jacob sent letters and gifts to his brother trying to win his good graces, but received no reply. The lack of response causes Jacob to become more afraid and he takes his family and his possessions and sends them ahead of him, and he stays behind alone. Now the bible doesn't say this, but I believe that Jacob wanted to be alone because he wanted to run again, but then a man suddenly appears and wrestles with Jacob until daybreak. The bible goes on to explain that after wrestling all night the man realized that he could not overpower Jacob, so instead of continuing to wrestle he struck Jacob's hip and knocked it out of joint at the socket. The scripture later reveals that the man who wrestled with Jacob was in fact God himself. When you replace the word "man" with the word "God" it puts an entirely different spin on this encounter. The bible is telling us that God sees that he cannot over power Jacob, and after hours of wrestling and struggling, God comes to the realization that Jacobs will to **run** is too strong for even Him to overcome.

Just as God wrestled with Jacob he is also willing to wrestle with you. He will attempt to grab your attention, pin down your flesh, contend against your reasons, and allow struggles in your decisions. God will attempt to battle you into submission, all with the intention of persuading you to stop running and stand. But you must understand that God will only attempt to keep you from running for so long before he will stop trying! Once God sees that Jacob is committed to running, God finally says "I'm done fighting with you"! _My friend, there are 2 words that you never want to hear the Lord speak over your life, and those 2 words are **"I'm done"**_!

God is Alpha and Omega, the beginning and the end. God is forever, so to hear him say "I'm done", means that he has chosen to stop placing his efforts, power and promises upon a person or thing. God told Jacob indirectly, I'm done wrestling with you. I'm done trying to get you to see things my way. I'm done trying to get you to trust me. I'm done trying to convince you that even though it doesn't feel right, you are in the right place at the right time.

I believe that Jacob had running faith. He believed God as long as things were safe, but the second the ground began to shake beneath him he started looking for the exits. God wrestling with Jacob was God's way of trying to get Jacob to change his running ways, but then God makes an interesting decision. He decides to break Jacob's leg. Jacob is a runner, so since Jacob won't trust God standing still, God breaks the thing that Jacob trusts in most...his leg. And my friend, the last thing I want to do is to scare you, but I have to be real with you. _Sometimes change is your only option and your last chance_. I'm sure that when God decided to stop fighting, Jacob felt some kind of relief, and then all of a sudden "snap"! His leg is gone. God tried to convince him not to run, but he would not listen, so now God makes it so that he cannot run! God gave Jacob a chance to trust and a chance to change, but when he sees that he couldn't change Jacob for the better spiritually he chose to change him for the worse physically.

Running is not worth the Risk

This book is titled "Change or Die", and I wrestled with the title because initially I thought it would be a bit harsh, but the reality is that change could very well mean life or death for you! Not just death in terms of the expiration of life; but if you look at Jacob, God had given him everything he promised him, but because he refused to change he put it all on the line. My friends, I believe that God wouldn't have you reading this book if the need to change did not hold the same type of weight in your life. God never addressed what Jacob had done to his brother. God looked past it and blessed Jacob anyway - and I'm sure that God has done the same for you. He doesn't talk to you about your past...not too much anyway. He made you a promise and he intends to keep it, even when you try to skate past the elephants in the room. *As much as God allows us to prosper in spite of our issues, there comes a point when God cannot allow you to go on the way that you are. He cannot continue to bless you as long as you continue to run from the things that you need to face*.

God tried to get Jacob to see things his way, and he just couldn't, so God has to break him down just to show him what happens when you refuse to trust. My friend, this is tough for me, but I must say that God has sent me as somebody's last warning. He sent me as his angel to wrestle with you; to convince you stop running, before God says "I'm done", and breaks you down! Please do not ignore this warning. I ask that you give heavy consideration to what I'm saying. Ask yourself these questions...

- ❖ What if this is really it?
- ❖ What if this is really my last opportunity to change the direction of my life?
- ❖ What if God has wrestled with me for the final time and is ready to leave me where he's found me?

Rather this is your last chance to change or not, *if you want change my friend; you MUST take on a new mind set. You have to tell yourself "this is it"*! I've been running and avoiding what I must face for years, and I know within my spirit - this is it for me! I can feel God getting tired of fighting with me. I can feel my greatest fears looming closer by the second. *If you really want change you have to be done giving yourself outs and options, and determine within your spirit that if "I don't change who I am, what I am, and where I am, I WILL DIE, who I am, what I am, and where I am"*!

After God breaks Jacob's leg, Jacob grabs a hold to the Lord, but the bible says that God commands Jacob to let him go, because the sun is coming up. God is preparing to leave Jacob to face his brother Esau alone with one leg. You must remember: *lack of change does not keep you from having to face your trials; it only keeps you from being prepared to face your trials when they come*! The only thing that fighting against change did for Jacob was to handicap him when it was time to face his issues. There is a time when the things that you've attempted to ignore are going to step out and look you in the eye and force you to deal with them one way or another. If you do not take advantage of the opportunity to change your running ways while the opportunity is present, you will not be ready to stand your ground when your opposition is present.

The "This Is It" Mentality

God broke Jacob's leg and then told him to let him go, God was going to leave him to face his issues as a broken man. But everything changes for Jacob when he refuses to let go of God. Broken, incapacitated, left alone with his enemy looming, and Jacob finally decides to change! Jacob, recognizing that he can no longer run, grabs hold to God and declares "I will not let go until you bless me"! _Part of establishing a "this is it" mentality means recognizing that you cannot let go_! While God wrestled with Jacob I'm sure that Jacob wanted God to let go of him, but now Jacob is recognizing that letting go of God, even prior to this instance, is what's gotten him into trouble.

God had already planned for Jacob to gain the birthright over his brother, even before their birth, but Jacob had "running faith", which would not allow him to wait on God. So, he and his mother devised a plan for him to get God's promise Jacob's way, on Jacob's terms, and in Jacob's timing. This plan, as you can see is now threatening to get Jacob killed! Jacob's plan to gain his promise through trickery instead of faith is where Jacob let go of God. Jacob also let go of God when he attempted to run from Esau after his father's death. But now he's broken and in a position where he says "this is it"; Esau is coming and he must be dealt with. It is at this point that Jacob recognizes that he can't afford to let go. Letting go will get him killed! Letting go will destroy his family, letting go will destroy his promise, and he now realizes that he **must** hold on because God is all he has!

Challenged to Change

This time I challenge you to have a conversation with yourself, in the presence of God. I challenge you to declare over yourself that "this is it"! No more running! No more putting off! No more avoiding and invading! *If you want to see change take place in your life you have no more opportunities to run*! Grab yourself in the collar, pound yourself on the chest, look yourself in the mirror and declare "this is it'! Change or Die! You must then declare that you will not let go until you are blessed! That's what's so special about Jacob's declaration. He didn't just declare to not let go, but he made sure to declare "I will not let go until you bless me"! You must take the same approach! You'd be surprised at how many people attempt to change but let it go before they began to see the fruits of their labor…but not you! You must resolve within yourself, and in the presence of God, that you intend to hold on to this process until the process blesses your life!

Before you put the book down, allow me to give you one added push. When Jacob grabbed hold of God and made this declaration, God was so impressed that he renames Jacob, and calls him Israel. God explains that he is changing his name because Jacob wrestled with God and Jacob won! How do you win against God? You show God so much faith and determination to hold on to his presence and his promise, until you compel him to give in to you! God says "because you submit to my will, you win! Because you recognize that you have no other option but to rely on me, you win! Because you are willing to grab a hold and not let go until you see a blessing, you win"!

Again, when you put down this book this time, declare that "this is it"! And then declare that you will not let go of this change until the change blesses your life! Make this declaration knowing that as you speak, God is declaring that you win! Before your Esau comes you've already won! Before your fight is finished you've already won! The victory is not in what you see; it comes by what you speak! Speak these words, get your victory, and then come back and talk to me in the next chapter!

Chapter 21

The Faith to Fix What's Been Broken

2 Signs of Broken Faith

In the last chapter I attempted to challenge you to fix your broken faith, but in order to fix something you must first be able to recognize when it's broken. There is no other group of people that exemplify broken faith better than the Israelites. Take a brief walk with me through their story in Exodus. I'd like to use this story to provide you with

Change or Die

pointers on how to recognize rather or not your faith is broken.

The Inability to Wait

Exodus 32:1, (NIV) - When the people saw that Moses was taking so long in coming down from the mountain, they gathered around Aaron and said; "Come, make us gods who will go before us. As for this fellow Moses who brought us up out of Egypt, we don't know what has happened to him."

This one scripture has 2 very important signs of broken faith. The first sign is *the inability to wait!* The bible says here that the Israelites saw that Moses was gone for "so long", but he was only gone for 40 days. These same people had been in Egypt for more than 400 years in slavery, and now they couldn't wait on Moses for 40 days. <u>You know that your faith is broken when you'd rather settle and be satisfied **now** than to wait on God and receive all of his promises **later**</u>. We are all human, and it is understandable to be anxious, especially when you feel that you're standing on the brink of something big. When your anxiousness gives way to frustration and reconsideration concerning the things that you have believed God for, "you are operating in broken faith".

If you are going to experience change, you must not just have faith, but your faith must be unwavering. *In order to maintain faith, you must learn that faith comes with a seat in a really uncomfortable waiting room*. God is a strategist, not a magician. A magician specializes in making things appear right before your eyes; but a strategist is an organizer and a planner. They specialize in moving pieces around until the puzzle comes together. This is how God operates. For example, when we ask him for a certain job we think that God could and should just give it to us on the spot. What we don't see is that God has to move a specific person into human resources who will select our resume. God has to put the right supervisor in place so that we can be chosen. He has to move someone else out of the positions that are just right for us. God knows exactly when you are going to ask, and since your blessing is brought by what comes out of your mouth, he has to line things up to be ready to move the day that you're ready to ask. He can't hold a job waiting on you to finish school, or to choose your career path, to stop wasting time and get serious about your life. But somehow, he maneuvers things around you so that the thing you ask for or the thing he promised can be ready for you at the appropriate time. God is awesome! Everything with him is strategic. He very seldom gives "snap of the finger blessings", but he moves with detailed timing and strategy. He somehow has the ability to link your movements and decisions to the movements and decisions of others, so that they can be in place to bless you at the appointed time. This is how God operates, and because your blessings depend on so many unseen and uncontrollable details, sometimes you will just have to wait…period.

Waiting Time is Not Wasted Time

While you are waiting, you must remember that it's what you do while you wait that makes all the difference. The bible says that the Israelites complained so much, that their journey through the wilderness, which should have only taken approximately 11 days, took 40 years! They spent more time complaining about what they had to deal with, rather than working through it and moving toward the next place. _Understand my friend, waiting is a part of faith, but waiting time is not wasted time, unless you waist it!!!_ Waiting time is supposed to be working time! Faith without works is dead! The worst thing that could happen to you is that God pulls back the curtain and you are not ready to perform! Your date is at the door and you're not prepared to leave. Your plane takes off in 10 minutes and your still in the security line. How can you pray for something and believe for something that you are not preparing to receive?

Remember this: _you don't always have to be prepared but you must always be preparing_!!! When it comes to my ministry I always feel like I'm ready. I'm ready for any stage, rather it be a homeless shelter or Lakewood Church! I always feel that no matter what stage, what area, or what place the Lord sends me - I can handle the assignment. Even though I feel this way I never allow that feeling to cause me to stop working. I very seldom preach purely from scripture and inspiration, instead, I write out the majority of my messages. I don't always need to write them, but to me, writing is working, and working is what puts faith into action. When I say it without writing it the words are gone after they come out of my mouth. If those words blessed someone, I can never bless someone else in that manor again because I didn't take time to write down the blessing.

When the words are written they can be spoken and have the ability to bless people over and over again. When I write, I can always revisit what I've written, and examine my growth. There are many messages that I've written years ago. When I read them today I find typos, misquotes, babbling, and points that were used to prolong the messages unnecessarily. At the time they were written, I felt like I could preach those messages anywhere, but now I see the need for correction. Revisiting those old messages causes me to thank God that he didn't allow me to take them to a grand stage. This is why it is important to keep working while you're waiting.

Just because you think you're ready does not always mean that you are; and believe it or not, some of us are stuck in a place that we can't get out of simply because we believe that we are ready to go higher right now. We don't want to wait any longer. We don't want to work anymore. We want our blessing right now! Let me tell you something my friend, _rushing God doesn't not make him move any faster_. Not preparing yourself for God's blessing because you think that you're already prepared does not open doors for you. I know it's frustrating to feel that you're ready for something that you have not received. I know that it's aggravating to watch others move ahead when you feel that you are just as capable as they are, and for that reason, it is a very real possibility that you have stopped attempting to change for the better... because you feel that change is getting you nowhere! This is what happens to the Israelites. They were released from slavery, but eventually desired to go back because they couldn't see how their "change" was better than their struggle. You may be frustrated with waiting, but believe me when I tell you - _your wait will only be prolonged by complaining_. Fussing with God, refusing to work on yourself, refusing to continue to prepare – these things will only make you more angry; and it will only make God more hesitant to bless you.

I challenge you to take advantage of your waiting time. Think of things that you still have yet to do. Consider the things that you haven't changed yet. After being given an opportunity to preach at my home church, which has a membership well over 2000, I had a friend once ask me "what is it like to preach in front of all of those people and have them shout over your message"? My response was this: "I don't think about making them shout; instead I think "what if I preach in front of 2000 people and they say nothing"? That has to be your mentality while you wait; not gaining an opportunity but being prepared to take full advantage of the opportunity when it comes your way! I know that you don't want to wait - nobody does - but there is a reason why God has you *here* instead of *there,* and it's not for you to sit around and waist time. You're not here to complain, nor are you here to wander in the wilderness. You are here so that you can *prepare to go there*!

What if it all changed today?

I challenge you to take a moment and think. Don't pray just yet, but think. Think about all of God's promises to you. Now consider this, if he gave them to you today would you really be able to handle them? This has nothing to do with money, but faithfully, emotionally, physically, and socially, would you be able to handle your destiny if God placed it in your life today? Let me help you with your answer - if you are complaining about what you have now, odds are you are not ready for what's coming. Why do I say that, because what's coming is greater than what's been! When has greater ever equaled easier? Never! God promised the Israelites a land flowing with milk and honey but he didn't tell them they would have to fight to obtain it. Why? Because if they couldn't pull themselves together enough to fight through the wilderness, how could they be ready to fight for a promise? Remember this: <u>*if you can't fight through a tough time, odds are, you won't fight to keep a good time. The struggle doesn't just bring you to a blessing but it prepares you to keep it once you have it in your hands*</u>.

The Unwillingness to Wait

The Israelite's first mistake was that they could not wait. *Their second mistake was that they were not willing to wait.* There is a difference. To not be "able" to wait is a *feeling*, but to not be "willing" to wait is a *decision*. These Israelites were not willing to wait and it cost them everything they built; it even cost some of them their lives. Instead of waiting for God's man (Moses) to come down, they took the closest thing to him, his brother Aaron. They then forced Aaron to satisfy their needs. They told Aaron that they wanted him to create a god for them, and Aaron did what they asked; but there was one problem. God hadn't called Aaron! Aaron was the one they chose, but Moses was the one that God had chosen for them. Broken faith will cause you to put Aaron where Moses should be, all because you are not willing to wait! Aaron was smart. He was Moses' interpreter. He was talented. He was the one who constructed the golden calf for the people. Aaron had attributes but he was not anointed. He was not the chosen man. He was accessible, he was impressionable, and he was easy to manipulate; which made him appealing to the people. So, when they decided they were done waiting on God, Aaron was the perfect person to lean on because he appeared to be the perfect replacement for Moses. *The quickest way to throw off your promise is to attempt to substitute what God has placed in your life.*

Broken faith will cause you to make substitutes instead of sacrifices.

The reason the Israelites asked Aaron to build a god, was so that they could claim their ways were inspired by some sort of divinity. My friend, please focus on God's WILL rather than your WANTS even when it feels like he's taking too long. Otherwise, you run the risk of doing as the Israelites did. You will substitute your Godly instructions for something or someone that takes your instructions, and then you will mask your decisions as God's instructions for your life.

Change Back!

Moses had gone into the mountain to obtain a word for the people. When Moses returns to the camp, and observed what they had done, he smashes the tablets that contained the word of God for their lives and he melted down the golden calf they had constructed. Not only were those Israelites forced to endure the destruction of what they had created, but Moses destroyed the word that they had been waiting for the whole time. On this road to change you must resolve within yourself that there are no substitutes. You cannot take the wheel from God just because you don't like how slow he's driving, and you cannot place someone in your life and make them what God did not intend for them to be. Aaron meant well, but he was operating out of place, and because of this he did more harm to the Israelites than good. Just because something is accessible does not mean that it is of God. Just because a person is willing does not mean that God is in favor of them. *Change for some simply means staying on course without wavering; accepting the way things are and believing that it's all working together for your good. I know that may seem contrary to change, but change for you may mean that you have to "change back" to your original state*. Change back to the person you were as you pressed toward the Red Sea - excited, trusting in God, not straying from the path! Change back to the person you were when God first brought you across the Red Sea - faithful, believing, ready for a new experience! Change back to the person you were before you became unwilling to wait on God – patient, understanding, and not easily aggravated.

Change means that you redirect, rearrange, recommit and reconstruct, but it also means that you take some time to revisit. There were things about you in the past that were beneficial, but life may have hit you so hard that you compromised or substituted. It is quite possible that you put Aaron where Moses should have been, simply because Aaron was there and he would give you what you wanted. Unfortunately Aaron hasn't made you better. Aaron hasn't lead you anywhere. Aaron hasn't given you anything that has not or could not be destroyed. What has substituting really gotten you? I am an advocate for making adjustments to a plan or a vision, but never substituting it.

Understanding the strain of change, I actually have compassion for the Israelites. Even though I don't agree with their actions I do understand their motives. They were in a new place, believing God for a new thing, and waiting for something that just didn't seem like it was coming. Most people in that predicament would feel like they have to do something, instead of just waiting. Being the pastor of a church is very tough, and I'd be lying if I told you that I've never considered giving up. But whenever I do, my wife reminds me of the vision for the church that I first shared with her. She would remind me of all of the wonderful plans and ideas the Lord had given me that I had not yet put into action. When I wanted to throw in the towel, in order to change my mind, she would take me back to the person I was in the past, before I became frustrated by my present. I challenge you to do the same, right now.

Challenged to Change

Take a moment, put down the book and think about "who you were before". Not the ugly parts of your past, but the beautiful pieces. Think about how excited you used to be, how willing to follow God you used to be, and how anxious you were to experience a new life through him. Really give it some thought. Maybe you used to want to go back to school - what happened? Maybe you used to have higher standards for who you allowed into your life - what happened? Maybe you used to know who you were, what you wanted, where you were going, and how you were getting there - what happened? Think about the "you" prior to the frustration, prior to the things that the world has done to you, prior to the hard times and struggle. In order to change your future you have to be able to remind yourself of who you were in your past. Think about it and then ask God to reignite that fire! Give you back that passion! Help you to become the person that looked struggle in the face and still believed for greater! Take some time, go back and get that person and then come back and let's continue our walk together!

Chapter 22

Change What Seems Harmless

God is Always Watching

Exodus 32:9, (NIV) - "I have seen these people," the LORD said to Moses, "and they are a stiff-necked people. Now leave me alone so that my anger may burn against them and that I may destroy them. Then I will make you into a great nation."

The Lord says something in this scripture that you must always consider as you go through the process of change, and those words are "I have seen these people". I truly believe that somehow these people believed that since Moses could not see them the Lord could not see them either. *Broken faith will give you the confidence to believe that God is not watching at all times. It will also cause you to believe that he will allow some things to slide just because he knows your heart and he knows what you're going through*.

This way of thinking is very deceptive in that it will cause you to be casual or even careless concerning God's word. A coworker once told me "it's better to ask for forgiveness than permission". That might work in the business world but not when it comes to God. **The bible tells us that obedience is better than sacrifice (1 Samuel 15:22)**. Permission can be granted or rejected without penalty, but forgiveness has a way of coming with lingering struggles. I know that we serve a forgiving God, *but broken faith seeks forgiveness, while strong faith seeks for fulfillment! Broken faith hopes that God isn't looking, but strong faith not only* *knows that God is looking and takes pride in giving God something good to see*! *If you are going to experience change you have to develop a mindset that says "you are tired of your faith only being used to get you out of trouble, and you want your faith to make you triumphant!!!*

Challenged to Change

I challenge you to examine the things in your life that you believe God may have allowed to slide in the past. This is not going to be easy because most of us only want to see God in a positive, forgiving light; but in order to change you must change your perception of God's perception. You must be cognizant of everything you do and how it "may" impact who you are trying to become.

Before you go into this challenge allow me to share something personal with you. I believe in the trinity (Father, Son and Holy Ghost). I preach and believe in the bible cover to cover. I believe in holiness, salvation, righteousness and separation from worldly behaviors. With that being said, I confess to you that I love R&B music; specifically the slow love songs. I have a playlist of nothing but slow love songs that I listen to from time to time when I need to mellow out, or when I'm on a date with my wife. For years I felt as if nothing was wrong with my playlist - after all, there is no cursing or vulgarity in the tracks that I've chosen. They all define the good of what I believe romantic love should represent. Be that as it may, I had to take out time to ensure that no song on that list insulted my Godly conviction. If there is cursing it is not on my list. If a song has a raunchy sexual undertone it is not on my list.

Because I considered every song on my list to be "harmless", I found myself listening to them without giving consideration to how God may have felt about my choice of music. God is unique, in that he is understanding but also jealous….very jealous! For me to give so much attention to something that did not "directly" lift God up, made me have to step back and really give credence to how it must have made him feel. Even with the songs being what I consider "clean", I had to take time to consider how often I listen to them in comparison to my gospel playlist. Those songs may not offend my conviction but they do not add to it or strengthen it either; and anything that does not strengthen you has very little to no value. So the question then became "how much time am I putting into something that has no value to who I am or where I'm going? How long do I continue listening and acting as if God is not present or impacted"?

I know it's going to be hard but I challenge you to take the time to examine your life in the same manor. Look at the things you do that may not be of value to you. Look at the things you consider harmless, but still may not be pleasing to God. Look at the things that you feel like you're getting away with. Things like gossiping, borrowing supplies from the job, telling little white lies every now and then. We all have something to examine and if I can admit mine to the world surely you can admit yours to yourself. Examine those little things that you do that you feel are harmless because those are the things that could be doing the most harm to you!

One more confession and then I promise we will get to the challenge! A few years ago, half of my bedroom ceiling caved in. This disaster caused hundreds of dollars worth of damage, and it was all caused by one small leak. The problem was not the leak itself, but that I ignored the leak over time. The more I ignored it the more it ate through the structure of the ceiling. Little by little, drop by drop, until one day it caused a great catastrophe! Just weeks prior to the ceiling caving in I had decided to move my bed to the other side of the room. The roof caved in at approximately 4am. Had the bed still been where it was previously, me, my wife and our small son would have been sleeping right below the area where the roof caved in. We could have been terribly hurt or worse. I praise God that in spite of my negligence, he still shielded my family. However, I still had a huge mess to clean up and a huge bill to pay, both of which could have been avoided.

Why am I asking you to examine the things that you take lightly? Because those are the things that do damage "over time". Little by little, drop by drop - and before you know it everything comes crashing down! *If you want to change you have to have a mind to handle small problems while they are small*. You cannot continue to ignore what you've been ignoring, operating as if God is fine with things that offend your conviction or add no value to who he intends for you to become. I never would have thought that small leak could have done so much damage; nor would I have thought that a leak that small could hurt the people love - but I was wrong. I don't want you to make the same mistake. I don't want your hopes, dreams and aspirations to come crashing down just because you ignored the small leaks in your life. I implore you, take this time, examine those things and just begin to make changes. It's easier to do a small repair than a major overhaul. Talk to God about those things. Make plans to repair those things, and then come back and continue our discussion in the next chapter.

Chapter 23

Setbacks Are Changes too...Be careful

Don't Break Your Word

Exodus 32:19, (NIV) - *"When Moses approached the camp and saw the calf and the dancing, his anger burned and he threw the tablets out of his hands, breaking them to pieces at the foot of the mountain".*

The broken faith of the people caused the word for their lives to be destroyed! Moses came out of the mountain with a hand engraved word, filled with blessings and promises from the Lord. But when he sees the broken faith of the people he threw that word down and destroyed it. They never heard it, never read it, and never got a chance to live it. As soon as Moses saw the way they were behaving he knew that they were not prepared to receive the word of God for their lives! The unique thing about this scripture to me is that God never told Moses to destroy the tablets, but God allowed Moses to destroy them. When your faith is broken your word runs the risk of being broken!

The day the Israelites started to turn was ironically just days before Moses came out of the mountain! *When your faith is broken it will cause you to give up right before your blessing comes*! Moses slammed down the tablets and broke them at the foot of the mountain – on the brink of reaching the people. *If you are going to experience change, you have to operate as if you are standing right on the brink of your change*! You have to take on the mindset, just as

Moses came down out of Mount Sinai; your change is coming down any moment now!

Notice vs. Focus

With Moses being high up in a mountain, for the people to see him coming down they had to be willing to consistently look up. Their focus would have had to be on something that was above their heads. The people lost their way when they became tired of *looking up* and instead they started *looking around*. <u>In order to truly experience change, you have to be willing to change what you're looking at. You must stop looking around and start looking up. Your change is not going to come from what's around you your change is coming from what's above you</u>!

Because your change comes from above, you have do as the bible says in **Colossians 3:2 (KJV), "set your affections on things above, not on things on this earth"**. <u>In order for you to really see the change you seek, your level of thinking and expectation must be raised to a higher level</u>.

Don't get me wrong, I realize that in order to change a situation you must recognize it, but you must understand the difference between "notice" and "focus". To *notice* is simply to observe or to be aware, but to *focus* means to center your interest and activity. To *focus* also means to adapt to the prevailing level of light and become able to see clearly! It's OK to notice, to observe, and to be aware of your surroundings; but in order to see change you must focus on things above. You must center your interest and activities on things that are above you. That means that everything you do has to work into your "ultimate plan". Even your short term struggles and circumstances must have a place in your long term goals.

Let me let you in on something; one of the reason people quit before they reach their goal is because they cannot allow themselves to see how their present situations can and will propel them to their next level. When I was a younger adult, starting my family, the only real jobs that I could seem to get were in retail management. I didn't need a degree, it paid what I thought at the time was good money, and it was the only profession that seemed to give me opportunities. Let me tell you, I **hated** retail management! The night shifts, the overnight shifts, the holidays, and the weekends made that profession almost unbearable. While people my age were out enjoying their youth I always seemed to be stuck at work. Remember earlier when I told you that I used to drive trucks? That passion was brought on by my desperation to get out of retail management. I tried on several occasions to quit for other jobs but I would always seem to find myself back in retail management...working the same position but for different companies.

For years, I tried to quit to no avail, and then I realized something. Retail didn't make it easy for me to have a "normal" working life, but it did make it easier for me to go back to school. Not having a set working schedule helped me to adjust my weeks to accommodate any class schedule. Also, because most retail stores are slow at night, it allowed me the opportunity to get my home work done on the clock....between working assignments of course (wink wink). I also noticed that the experiences I'd gained from retail management qualified me for better jobs; I just needed a degree to meet the educational requirements. So, I made a decision. Instead of trying to get out of retail, I used it to prepare me to go to my next level. I had been going to school part time, here and there for years, but I decided that I would work fulltime and go to school full time - with no semesters off. I had been going to school part time for more than 8 years, but when I started going full-time, I completed the remainder of my Associates and my Bachelor's Degrees in just over 2 years! Did you get that math? Because my focus was on things around me I wandered around in school for 8 years - a class here, a class there; but when I began to focus on things above, I finished approximately 100 credit hours of school in just over 2 years.

Not 3 months after receiving my bachelor's degree I was offered a position at Blue Cross Blue Shield - making more money, working day shifts, no weekends or holidays, with paid overtime! When my focus was just on being stuck in retail; I could not get out of retail. But when I began to focus on achieving a higher education, so that I could obtain higher pay, better benefits, and a more ideal career, it happened in little to no time. The ironic thing is that without those years in retail I may have never been hired into health care. I was able to pull from my bad past experiences to qualify me for a new better experience, because I stopped focusing on what retail was doing to me and started noticing what retail could do for me.

Challenged to Change

I challenge you to take some time and examine the things that presently has your focus. Ask yourself, are you focused on things above you or things around you? If you discover that you are focused on the things around you, you will also discover that you are either not rising above them or you are rising very slowly. I challenge you to write down what it is you want out of life. Determine where it is you want to go. Resolve within yourself what you believe you are supposed to have and commit to focusing on it with an intense passion! If you see somebody who has what you want, talk to them about how they got it. If you know that there is a house you want, go to the bank and find out what it would take for you to get approved. Print out your credit report, and if your score is not what you need it to be draw up a plan and a time frame to get it fixed. Notice the low score, but focus on bring it higher! This *"focus over notice"* principle must be applied to every area of change that you seek for your life. I know I've said this before, but this is a pivotal part of change - one that you must do!

You have to change your *focus*. In order to do this you have to force yourself to *notice* the things below and *focus* on things above. It's not easy, because the things below are closer to you; they can touch you, push you, speak to you, and throw negative things directly into your view. I challenge you to take a few moments and look up! Pull your chin out of your chest. Stop looking down and around at things in your life that you cannot handle. Put down the book and deal with yourself for a few moments. <u>Tell yourself "from this point on I'm looking up</u>! I may notice what's around me but I will focus on what's above me"! Pray for God to give you the strength to do this consistently, and then come back and talk to me a little more...we're almost done!

CHANGE or DIE

PART 6

THE RESULTS OF CHANGE

Chapter 24

The Moving Pieces of Change

Get Off of the Wall

Let's go back to **2 Kings Chapter 6 (KJV)**. The woman approaches the king and reveals what she has done. He immediately rips his clothes and makes a vow. The king has been praying and believing God, but the bible says that he is walking on a wall. A wall never leads to a new place, but it separates one place from another. Yes, the king has been praying and he's been waiting; but he's been doing this while pacing back and forth along the wall. If you want change my friend, you have got to get off the wall! The wall, as I am describing it, is a divided mindset - where you long for the future ahead but you cannot leave the past behind. When you understand what you must do, but you continuously rationalize the reasons not to do it. Remember: **God is not the author of confusion (1 Cor 14:33, KJV), and a house divided against its self cannot stand (Mk 3:25, KJV).** *If you want to see change take place in your life, you have got to stop standing between where you are and where you're destined to be. Make up your mind to move forward and get yourself of the wall*!

Still not grasping the concept of getting off of the wall? Allow me to approach this in a different way. Here in the bible, we are talking about the king of Israel, but there is another king that you may be familiar with; he was called the King of Pop, none other than Michael Jackson. Even in death, Michael Jackson is arguable the biggest star of any genre of music this world has ever seen. But before he became a megastar he was simply little Michael Jackson of the Jackson 5. He wanted to leave his brothers and go off on his own, but for a while he could not do it because he

Change or Die

was torn between what he was and what he wanted to become. After years of struggle and toil, he finally left his brothers and created an album that would change the landscape of music forever, an album entitle Thriller! The Thriller album won 8 Grammy's in 1984 and went on to sell more than 100 million copies worldwide. Thriller made Michael Jackson the biggest name in the world and gave him riches that he never amassed while together with his brothers, but Thriller was not Michael Jackson's first solo project. Thriller was his biggest, brightest and best, but Michael Jackson did not create Thriller until after he created his first album, which was entitled "Off The Wall"!

"Off The Wall" was the album that signified his exit from standing on the divide between his present and his destiny. He went on to become the greatest, but that did not happen until after he got "off the wall"! Michael Jackson went from "Off the Wall" to "Thriller", and God sent me here to tell you if you think Michael Jackson's success was a thriller wait until you get a look at the plans he has for you! My friend I truly believe that eyes have not seen, ears have not heard, neither has it entered into the heart of man, the great CHANGE that God is about to perform in your life!

But before you can see this wonderful change, you must stop standing in the divide, behaving as if you cannot move from where you are. You must look at the wall in your life and believe that it is not too high to get over, or too low to get under, and most importantly, you cannot allow yourself to stay stuck in the middle! Before you can change, you must first believe that you can! You can do this! You can overcome odds, walk away from bad people, break away from addiction, start a business, finish school, change bad habits and behaviors - but first you have got to get off of that wall in your life that is separating who and where you are from whom and where you should be!

The Discomfort of Change

We're still in 2 Kings 6 and the report of this woman, has troubled the king so much that he comes down off of the wall; but not before making a vow to take the life of the Prophet Elisha. Yes, the king has been praying and believing, but it appears that the king has forsaken his faith and decided to take matters into his own hands. Elisha is the one that told him to let these people go, and now they have come back and caused this great famine. So the king, out of anger and frustration declares; "may God do this to me and more if I let this man live beyond today"! The king was *mad, hurt*, and *confused*. He was *mad* because he chose God over what he wanted. *Hurt* because he believed God to change the terrible outcome, but it seems to be getting worse. *Confused* because he believed Elisha would guide him and instead, everyone is suffering. So the king snaps for a second, and says I can't just sit back and let this happen, I've got to do something!

I wonder if you've ever been angry because you trusted God with your whole heart; but what you've trusted him for just doesn't seem to be working out? Have you ever been hurt because you believed that even though things were tight, God was going to open a door; but you're still waiting on that door to open? Have you ever been confused because you thought that God sent someone into your life to guide you and to make you better; but because of that person you are now worse off than you were before? Those things left you wondering; "Why am I trying to do things better and things just keep getting worse"?

A hard truth about change is that it has the potential to bring some uncomfortable – even ungodly feelings out of you! Even when you're a devout Christian and you love the Lord with all your heart; change will still cause you to lash out in anger or frustration, or even shut down and not want to talk to anyone. We have mastered being able to look happy and be miserable at the same time; but when you really decide that you are ready for something different; the amount of sacrifice, waiting, resistance and opposition you have to deal with from people and uncontrollable situations has the potential to bring some unusual behavior out of you. I have to tell you this so that you don't quit on change; because there will be days when the process of change will make you feel like you just can't take any more. If you're not careful you will take on the same attitude as the king. You will develop a vengeful heart and began to declare war and seek vengeance, instead of speaking peace and claiming victory.

Prayer in the Mist of Change!

Change takes patience, but it also has the ability to take away patience. Change will drive you up the wall. Change *will cause you to attempt to force the future to happen at your desired speed. Change will cause you to feel like changing isn't worth the agony associated with it.* As we loom closer to the end of our conversation, this time I'm not going to ask you to stop and pray. Instead, I'd like to ask if you would allow me to pray for you! The journey to the change that you seek is not going to be an easy road. The waiting and suffering associated with it is going to provoke you and tempt you to make decisions that could be costly to your destiny. So, if you would allow me, before we go any further; **I would like to pray for you as Jesus prayed for Simon in Luke, 22:32 (KJV). In this scripture Jesus prays that Simon's** *faith does not fail.* Jesus' reason for praying these specific words is because he sees the road ahead for Simon and knows that it will be tougher to walk than Simon realizes. My friend, if you would allow me, I would like to pray the same prayer over you right now. *As you walk this journey that leads to the greatest change you've ever experienced in your life, I pray that your faith does not fail you! Your patience will fail you, your intelligence will fail you, your temper will fail you, your physical and mental capabilities will fail you, but as long as* your faith stays intact, you will have everything you need to pull yourself back in line.

Jesus told Simon Peter that Satan looked to sift him as wheat, and my friend allow me to inform you that Satan looks to do the same to you. Sift means to test, to examine or to scrutinize. *As you walk this path to change, Satan looks to test your patience, to examine your abilities, and to scrutinize your every move*. He is going to badger you nonstop. He is going to do everything in his power to convince you that you will not find the change that you seek. He is going to tell you that everything God has told you has been a lie, and nothing that you've been working for is coming to you. He's going to constantly throw the achievements of others into your face as a reminder of what you don't have and will never achieve. That is why I pray that your faith does not fail; *once you begin to pursue change, your faith is going to be the only thing you can truly depend on.* I pray that your faith keeps you grounded, focused, and inspired. I pray that your faith keeps you moving forward until all of your dreams, goals and promises are realized. These and greater things I pray for your life, in Jesus' name, amen!

Change the Blame

The king convinces himself that Elisha has done this. Elisha was the one that caused him to make what he thought was a stupid decision. Elisha was the one that he trusted, and Elisha is the one that has to pay! I wonder if you've ever had an Elisha in your life. Whenever things aren't going the way that we plan there is always an Elisha for us to place the blame on. The king trusted Elisha when there was nothing on the line, but now that things are tough he turns on Elisha. Here is another truth about change that I need you to remember: *the stress, frustration and aggravation associated with change can cause you to turn on the people you trust.* If not handled appropriately, change can cause you to turn on the people who only mean the best for you. We are cautious of enemies posing as friends, but if you want change; you must recognize *you are dealing with a devil that has a talent for making friends look like enemies.*

If you give it some thought, you would probably have to admit that this is one of the biggest reasons that you have made mistakes in your life. You listened to everyone except for the people that cared for you the most. There is somebody reading this book that has shut somebody off who you may need down the line. There is somebody out there who has been listening to the wrong people; because the words of the wrong people always seem to give us a "right" feeling. The person that's best for you is usually the person that will both scold you and protect you. If you have a person in your life that will only do one or the other I strongly urge you to examine that relationship. *If you want change, you must stop making attempts to only be around people who agree with you*. The most important people to you during your process are those who will tell you where you fall short, and then help you to fill in those gaps. They will tell you that you are making a fool of yourself in private, so that you can give the best presentation of yourself in public.

You must let go of the thinking that the people who tell you the hard truths are jealous, ruling or manipulative. *If you are going to change, you need someone in your life that's going to tell you what's right even when you don't want to hear it*! This is a vital step within the process. You must remember that no person can be great all by themselves. Most great men or women will be the first to tell you that they are only great because they are standing on the shoulders of someone else. People won't have your same gifts, but they will have things that you don't possess. Some people can make money but they can't budget it. Some can speak or sing, but they can't write a song or speech. *If you are going to change, you are always going to need somebody...not everybody...but "somebody" who can do the work in the shadows so that you can shine in the spotlight.*

In the early stages of my ministry, I would focus so much on the number of people who attended my service. If the numbers were not to my liking I would become very upset. It wasn't until I started to focus more on the vision that God gave me for the ministry that I learned to concern myself more with the people I already had, instead of those who were not yet connected. When we were blessed to find our present church home it was a larger administrative building that had not been utilized in more than 3 years. The conditions were not suitable for occupation and I could not afford, nor did the church have the money to pay for all of the needed expense. Without having to be asked the membership stepped up. They put forth their extra monies, time and efforts to turn that building into a beautiful place of worship! Most people want to be a part of greatness, but very few are willing to build something great! I thank the Lord for sending me a group of people that are excited to be a part of the building process!

Challenged to Change

I challenge you to put down the book yet again, just for a few moments and pray. This time I want you to pray that the Lord would send the right people in your direction. Pray that God will send you builders, laborers, and supporters. Pray for people that will buy into your gifts and talents. Take a little time; envision the type of people you will need to obtain and maintain the desired changes in your life. Picture them, pray for them, and then come back and see me in the next chapter.

Chapter 25

Change is Closer than You Think!

Let's return to the end of **2 Kings Chapter 6 (KJV)**, where the king goes to keep his word and take the life of Elisha. When he arrives at the place where Elisha is, the king reveals his true feelings in verse 33. He says, "This disaster is from the Lord". All of this fuss about killing Elisha just to find out that Elisha wasn't his problem. The king's issue was that he had been praying and believing, and the Lord had not yet changed his situation. So then, he says something that you must avoid saying and feeling at all cost; the king declares, "Why should I wait on God any longer"? Here is the most important thing you must remember about change, and I believe God sent me here to tell you this: **<u>the day you decide to give up on change, is the day before change is going to happen</u>**! The day that you decide to give up on change is the day before the blessing connected to your change will take effect! This has to be your mentality; you must believe it to be true.

The king of Israel declares "the Lord has brought about this struggle; why should I wait on him any longer"? That is the last sentence in the Chapter 6. At the start of the 7th chapter Elisha responds by saying "hear this, the word of the Lord; thus saith the Lord, tomorrow about this time shall a measure of fine flour be sold for a shekel, and two measures of barley for a shekel, in the gate of Samaria". In other words, on the day that the King was ready to give up on change the prophet lets him know that *tomorrow* is the day that everything is about to change!

When you're going through your change you're going to feel that you hate the suffering, and you can't stand the pain; you're going to feel that you are so tired of going through that you are just fed up; but you can't give up on this! *In order to experience change, you must tell yourself daily "I am only a day away. The day that I stop seeking, is the day before I finally find what I've been looking for. Quitting now is not only out of the question, but it doesn't make sense, because I'm only one day away"*!

Pursue the Possibility of Change

In chapter 7, after Elisha promises the king that things will change in just 24 hours, the bible switches gears to the 4 men that would bring about this miraculous change. These 4 men were "leprous". They were sick from the inside out; standing at the point of death. So they examined where they were, not just geographically but where they were in their lives as a whole. They said to one another, *"if we sit still here, we are going to die"*. If they stay where they were, if they continue doing the things they've been doing, if they continue to use their condition as a reason to stay put; these 4 men decided that if they do not **change** they will **die**! When we speak about changing our lives we have a tendency to see ourselves living better than we are now. But have you ever really ever looked at your life and said if I don't do something about my present situation I'm going to die broke, lonely, angry or an underachiever? If you've never thought along these lines, I come to tell you that you must. *In order to change, you must see yourself dying just as you are. You must consider all of the things that you are missing out on, all of the time that you've allowed to pass, all of the excuses that you've made - and most importantly, you must see yourself dying before you have the opportunity to change those things*!

These lepers knew that dying as they were was a certainty, so they said "if we go beyond the gate, where the Syrians are, maybe they will kill us, maybe they will let us live, but we know that surely, if we stay here we are going to die". So they moved toward the Syrians, and the bible says that once they came into the camp of Syria everyone was gone. Not only were the Syrians gone, but they left behind all of the food, drinks, money, supplies - and all of the silver and gold that they possessed! The bible says that Syria fled, because the Lord caused them to hear a great army moving in their direction. The footsteps of this great army they thought they heard, was nothing more than the footsteps of those 4 sick lepers! *My friend, when you start moving toward your change all that you will see is you; but God will dispatch an army of angels that will move in succession with your footsteps!*

Sick of being...

When the 4 Lepers came into the Syrians camp, the bible says that they ate, drank and packed up silver, gold and raiment; and went and hid their portion for themselves. They then went and shared the news of what they had found with those others who had been suffering through the famine. They were just 4 sick individuals with nothing to lose and nothing to look forward to; but because they decided to change, they were not only the first to experience this great victory, but they were given the ability to choose all that they wanted! *The people who get the most out of change are the people who are sick of being where they are at the present time*! It's that sick feeling that has to drive you to move toward something greater.

The bible says that the 4 lepers consumed as much food and drink as they could, which I understand; but it also says that they took and hid for themselves both silver and gold! What good is silver and gold to 4 individuals who are deathly ill? I believe they hid these treasures because they were no longer expecting to die! The change that they pursued, based on the difficulties of life, caused them to take on a new outlook on life. It is amazing to me that not one of the lepers reminded the rest that silver and gold would be useless to them, but once they came in contact with it they all began to store it away for themselves without consideration of death. Their thinking and behaviors became new. They were no longer 4 sick men looking for a crust of bread; they were now 4 wealthy men who were making plans to continue to change and enjoy the remainder of their days! *This is what change does for you...it gives you a new outlook on life! It rejuvenates you naturally, spiritually, mentally and financially! It gives you more to look forward to. Most importantly, it shows you that you can overcome and succeed, no matter what comes your way*! Remember, the Lepers still have Leprosy; but they are not allowing their sickness to keep them from changing their lives. They have no intention of going back to the roadside, no intention of ever being hungry again, and no intention of ever being homeless, having to beg or being afraid ever again. Because they were willing to pursue change, they now had the resources to live the life that they were promised!

Anybody, Anything, Any Person Can Be Changed

These lepers embody every obstacle that we face today. They were physically ill and facing death. Doctors could do nothing to cure them. They were only surrounded by one another, which meant that they had only sick people around them. They were outcasts, and lived in fear of death at the hands of their enemies. They were poor and had no place to live. These 4 men had absolutely nothing going for themselves, and it was their realization of this that prompted them to move toward change! Their mindset was simply this, "we MAY die if we move, but we WILL die if we don't". And because they were willing to face death, rejection, harm and humiliation, the Lord made sure that by the time they made it to their destination; everything was in place and waiting for them!

Chapter 26

Choose to Change

In Conclusion

My friend, I believe that your predestined outcome is either the same or even greater than that of these 4 Lepers. I believe that the key to everything you've been wanting out of life is in your refusal to die where you are! You are no worse off right now than these 4 Lepers, and if they can pick themselves up and be willing to face challenges just to achieve change, I know that you can as well! I believe that there is a great supply of health, wealth and resources waiting for you. All you have to do is move toward them. As I've said previously, the road won't be easy; but the good thing is that the road is the toughest part! Can you imagine the fear and discomfort the Lepers must have felt coming closer and closer to Syria; just to find that everything they had been afraid of had been chased away before they even arrived? <u>My friend, **this is change**! It's a road that makes you feel afraid, weary, worn and uncomfortable. You know what you want to see - but you don't know what to expect. You know what you want to gain - but you don't know what lies in waiting. And then, after all of your work and your worry, your pain and your pressing; you arrive to find that all of your fears have been chased away! Not only are you given more of what you asked for, but the Lord throws in some things that you didn't ask for!</u>

The Lepers only wanted a little bit of food, but once they arrived the Lord gave them enough food to feed the masses and enough wealth to restore the economy of a nation! Do you remember the prophecy given by Elijah when the king came to kill him? It was all brought to pass by the willingness of these lepers to pursue change! They were not only able to change their own lives, but they changed the lives of everyone around them! Imagine my friend, that you are one change away from having this type of impact. One step away from changing not only your life or the lives of your loved ones, but changing the lives of people that you don't even know! Moving from where you are now could mean you changing lives, finances, communities, cities, countries...even the world! The alternative is to stay where you are... and die.

One Last Challenge!

My friend, I have one last challenge for you that will determine rather or not you are prepared. Open your eyes and look around you. Take a look at every aspect of your life. Your relationships, health, strength, bank account, education, home, salary, marriage, credit...everything ...do you see it? Now, close your eyes and look at everything you could have! Everything you could do! Everything you could be! Look at everything you desire! Everything you believe you should have! What you see when your eyes are closed are the things that you can have by faith, but you must be willing to make the necessary changes. Before you open your eyes, I challenge you to make a choice. Change is a *choice*; either you choose to embrace it, or you choose to stay as you are. The 4 Lepers moved based on a "possibility". They had no guarantee that things would work out the way they did; but they were willing to pursue the possibility. My friend, I have been inspired by God to write this entire book just to give one very clear challenge...**pursue your possibilities (change), or except your realities (die)**.

Put the book down, take me up on my last challenge, and remember do not open your eyes until you've made a choice! **Change or Die**.

Printed in Great Britain
by Amazon